Krapp's Last Tape

AND OTHER DRAMATIC PIECES

D0377490

Works by Samuel Beckett published by Grove Press

COLLECTED POEMS IN ENGLISH AND FRENCH

COLLECTED SHORTER PLAYS
(All That Fall, Act Without Words I, Act Without Words II, Krapp's Last Tape,
Rough for Theatre I, Rough For Theatre II, Embers, Rough for Radio I, Rough
for Radio II, Words and Music, Cascando, Play, Film, The Old Tune, Come
and Go, Eh Joe, Breath, Not I, That Time, Footfalls, Ghost Trio, . . . but the
clouds . . . , A Piece of Monologue, Rockaby, Ohio Impromptu, Quad,
Catastrophe, Nacht and Träume, What Where)

COMPLETE SHORT PROSE: 1929–1989
(Assumption, Sedendo et Quiescendo, Text, A Case in a Thousand, First
Love, The Expelled, The Calmative, The End, Texts for Nothing 1–13, From an
Abandoned Work, The Image, All Strange Away, Imagination Dead Imagine,
Enough, Ping, Lessness, The Lost Ones, Fizzles 1–8, Heard in the Dark 1,
Heard in the Dark 2, One Evening, As the story was told, The Cliff, neither,
Stirrings Still, Variations on a "Still" Point, *Faux Départs*, The Capital of
the Ruins)

DISJECTA:
Miscellaneous Writings and
a Dramatic Fragment

ENDGAME AND ACT WITHOUT
WORDS

HAPPY DAYS

HOW IT IS

I CAN'T GO ON, I'LL GO ON:
A Samuel Beckett Reader

KRAPP'S LAST TAPE (All That Fall,
Embers, Act Without Words I,
Act Without Words II)

MERCIER AND CAMIER

MOLLOY

MORE PRICKS THAN KICKS
(Dante and the Lobster, Fingal,
Ding-Dong, A Wet Night,
Love and Lethe, Walking Out,
What a Misfortune,
The Smeraldina's Billet Dòux,
Yellow, Draff)

MURPHY

NOHOW ON (Company,
Ill Seen Ill Said, Worstward Ho)

PROUST

STORIES AND TEXTS FOR NOTHING
(The Expelled, The Calmative,
The End, Texts for Nothing 1–13)

THREE NOVELS (Molloy,
Malone Dies, The Unnamable)

WAITING FOR GODOT

WATT

HAPPY DAYS:
Production Notebooks

WAITING FOR GODOT:
Theatrical Notebooks

SAMUEL BECKETT

Krapp's Last Tape

AND OTHER DRAMATIC PIECES

GROVE PRESS
NEW YORK

Copyright © 1957 by Samuel Beckett
Copyright © 1958, 1959, 1960 by Grove Press, Inc.

All rights reserved. No part of this book may be reproduced in any form or by any electronic or mechanical means, including information storage and retrieval systems, without permission in writing from the publisher, except by a reviewer, who may quote brief passages in a review. Any members of educational institutions wishing to photocopy part or all of the work for classroom use, or publishers who would like to obtain permission to include the work in an anthology, should send their inquiries to Grove/Atlantic, Inc., 841 Broadway, New York, NY 10003.

CAUTION: Professionals and amateurs are hereby warned that *Krapp's Last Tape, All That Fall, Embers, Act Without Words I,* and *Act Without Words II* are subject to a royalty. They are fully protected under the copyright laws of the United States, Canada, United Kingdom, and all British Commonwealth countries, and all countries covered by the International Copyright Union, the Pan-American Copyright Convention, and the Universal Copyright Convention. All rights, including professional, amateur, motion picture, recitation, public reading, radio broadcasting, television, video or sound taping, all other forms of mechanical or electronic reproduction, such as information storage and retrieval systems and photocopying, and rights of translation into foreign languages, are strictly reserved.

Stock and amateur applications to perform *Krapp's Last Tape, Act Without Words I,* and *Act Without Words II*, and those other rights stated above, must be made in advance, before rehearsals begin, with Samuel French, Inc. 45 West 25th Street, New York, NY 10010; for all other rights, apply to Georges Borchardt, 136 East 57th Street, New York, NY 10022. For *Embers* and *All That Fall*, all inquiries should be addressed to Georges Borchardt.

Published simultaneously in Canada
Printed in the United States of America

Library of Congress Catalog Card Number 60-8388
ISBN 0-8021-5134-5 (pbk.)

Grove Press
an imprint of Grove/Atlantic, Inc.
841 Broadway
New York, NY 10003

Distributed by Publishers Group West

www.groveatlantic.com

08 09 10 11 12   42 41 40 39 38 37 36

CONTENTS

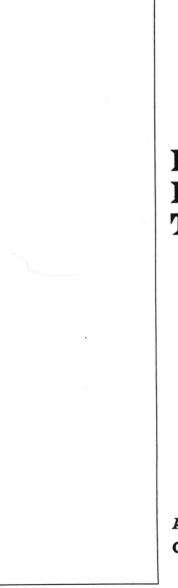

Krapp's
Last
Tape

**A PLAY IN
ONE ACT**

Krapp's Last Tape was first performed at the
Royal Court Theatre in London on October 28, 1958.
It was directed by Donald McWhinnie and
played by Patrick Magee.

A late evening in the future.

Krapp's den.

Front centre a small table, the two drawers of which open towards audience.

Sitting at the table, facing front, i.e. across from the drawers, a wearish old man: Krapp.

Rusty black narrow trousers too short for him. Rusty black sleeveless waistcoat, four capacious pockets. Heavy silver watch and chain. Grimy white shirt open at neck, no collar. Surprising pair of dirty white boots, size ten at least, very narrow and pointed.

White face. Purple nose. Disordered grey hair. Unshaven.

Very near-sighted (but unspectacled). Hard of hearing.

Cracked voice. Distinctive intonation.

Laborious walk.

On the table a tape-recorder with microphone and a number of cardboard boxes containing reels of recorded tapes.

Table and immediately adjacent area in strong white light. Rest of stage in darkness.

Krapp remains a moment motionless, heaves a great sigh, looks at his watch, fumbles in his pockets, takes out an envelope, puts it back, fumbles, takes out a small bunch of keys, raises it to his eyes, chooses a key, gets up and moves to front of table. He stoops, unlocks first drawer, peers into it, feels about inside it, takes out a reel of tape, peers at it, puts it back, locks drawer, unlocks second drawer, peers into it, feels about inside it, takes out a large banana, peers at it, locks drawer, puts keys back in his pocket. He turns, advances to edge of stage, halts, strokes banana, peels it, drops skin at his feet, puts end of banana

*in his mouth and remains motionless,
staring vacuously before him. Finally he
bites off the end, turns aside and begins
pacing to and fro at edge of stage, in the
light, i.e. not more than four or five paces
either way, meditatively eating banana.
He treads on skin, slips, nearly falls,
recovers himself, stoops and peers at skin
and finally pushes it, still stooping, with his
foot over the edge of stage into pit. He
resumes his pacing, finishes banana,
returns to table, sits down, remains a
moment motionless, heaves a great sigh,
takes keys from his pockets, raises them to
his eyes, chooses key, gets up and moves
to front of table, unlocks second drawer,
takes out a second large banana, peers at
it, locks drawer, puts back keys in his
pocket, turns, advances to edge of stage,
halts, strokes banana, peels it, tosses skin
into pit, puts end of banana in his mouth
and remains motionless, staring vacuously
before him. Finally he has an idea, puts
banana in his waistcoat pocket, the end
emerging, and goes with all the speed he*

*can muster backstage into darkness. Ten
seconds. Loud pop of cork. Fifteen
seconds. He comes back into light carrying
an old ledger and sits down at table. He
lays ledger on table, wipes his mouth,
wipes his hands on the front of his
waistcoat, brings them smartly together
and rubs them.*

KRAPP   (*briskly*). Ah! (*He bends over ledger, turns
the pages, finds the entry he wants, reads.*)
Box . . . thrree . . . spool . . . five. (*He raises
his head and stares front. With relish.*)
Spool! (*Pause.*) Spooool! (*Happy smile.
Pause. He bends over table, starts peering
and poking at the boxes.*) Box . . . thrree
. . . thrree . . . four . . . two . . . (*with
surprise*) nine! good God! . . . seven . . . ah!
the little rascal! (*He takes up box, peers at
it.*) Box thrree. (*He lays it on table, opens
it and peers at spools inside.*) Spool . . . (*he
peers at ledger*) . . . five . . . (*he peers at
spools*) . . . five . . . five . . . ah! the little
scoundrel! (*He takes out a spool, peers at
it.*) Spool five. (*He lays it on table, closes*

box three, puts it back with the others, takes up the spool.) Box thrree, spool five. (*He bends over the machine, looks up. With relish.*) Spooool! (*Happy smile. He bends, loads spool on machine, rubs his hands.*) Ah! (*He peers at ledger, reads entry at foot of page.*) Mother at rest at last ... Hm ... The black ball ... (*He raises his head, stares blankly front. Puzzled.*) Black ball? ... (*He peers again at ledger, reads.*) The dark nurse ... (*He raises his head, broods, peers again at ledger, reads.*) Slight improvement in bowel condition ... Hm ... Memorable ... what? (*He peers closer.*) Equinox, memorable equinox. (*He raises his head, stares blankly front. Puzzled.*) Memorable equinox? ... (*Pause. He shrugs his shoulders, peers again at ledger, reads.*) Farewell to—(*he turns the page*)—love.

He raises his head, broods, bends over machine, switches on and assumes listening posture, i.e. leaning forward, elbows on table, hand cupping ear towards machine, face front.

TAPE   (*strong voice, rather pompous, clearly
        Krapp's at a much earlier time.*) Thirty-
        nine today, sound as a—(*Settling himself
        more comfortably he knocks one of the
        boxes off the table, curses, switches off,
        sweeps boxes and ledger violently to the
        ground, winds tape back to beginning,
        switches on, resumes posture.*) Thirty-
        nine today, sound as a bell, apart from my
        old weakness, and intellectually I have
        now every reason to suspect at the . . .
        (*hesitates*) . . . crest of the wave—or
        thereabouts. Celebrated the awful
        occasion, as in recent years, quietly at the
        Winehouse. Not a soul. Sat before the fire
        with closed eyes, separating the grain from
        the husks. Jotted down a few notes, on the
        back of an envelope. Good to be back in
        my den, in my old rags. Have just eaten I
        regret to say three bananas and only with
        difficulty refrained from a fourth. Fatal
        things for a man with my condition.
        (*Vehemently.*) Cut 'em out! (*Pause.*) The
        new light above my table is a great
        improvement. With all this darkness round

me I feel less alone. (*Pause.*) In a way.
(*Pause.*) I love to get up and move about
in it, then back here to . . . (*hesitates*) . . .
me. (*Pause.*) Krapp.

Pause.

The grain, now what I wonder do I mean
by that, I mean . . . (*hesitates*) . . . I suppose
I mean those things worth having when all
the dust has—when all *my* dust has settled.
I close my eyes and try and imagine them.

Pause. Krapp closes his eyes briefly.

Extraordinary silence this evening, I strain
my ears and do not hear a sound. Old Miss
McGlome always sings at this hour. But
not tonight. Songs of her girlhood, she says.
Hard to think of her as a girl. Wonderful
woman though. Connaught, I fancy.
(*Pause.*) Shall I sing when I am her age, if
I ever am? No. (*Pause.*) Did I sing as a
boy? No. (*Pause.*) Did I ever sing? No.

Pause.

Just been listening to an old year, passages
at random. I did not check in the book, but

it must be at least ten or twelve years ago.
At that time I think I was still living on
and off with Bianca in Kedar Street. Well
out of that, Jesus yes! Hopeless business.
(*Pause.*) Not much about her, apart from
a tribute to her eyes. Very warm. I
suddenly saw them again. (*Pause.*)
Incomparable! (*Pause.*) Ah well . . .
(*Pause.*) These old P.M.s are gruesome, but
I often find them—(*Krapp switches off,
broods, switches on*)—a help before
embarking on a new . . . (*hesitates*) . . .
retrospect. Hard to believe I was ever that
young whelp. The voice! Jesus! And the
aspirations! (*Brief laugh in which Krapp
joins.*) And the resolutions! (*Brief laugh in
which Krapp joins.*) To drink less, in
particular. (*Brief laugh of Krapp alone.*)
Statistics. Seventeen hundred hours, out of
the preceding eight thousand odd,
consumed on licensed premises alone.
More than 20%, say 40% of his waking
life. (*Pause.*) Plans for a less . . . (*hesitates*)
. . . engrossing sexual life. Last illness of his
father. Flagging pursuit of happiness.

Unattainable laxation. Sneers at what he calls his youth and thanks to God that it's over. (*Pause.*) False ring there. (*Pause.*) Shadows of the opus . . . magnum. Closing with a—(*brief laugh*)—yelp to Providence. (*Prolonged laugh in which Krapp joins.*) What remains of all that misery? A girl in a shabby green coat, on a railway-station platform? No?

Pause.

When I look—

Krapp switches off, broods, looks at his watch, gets up, goes backstage into darkness. Ten seconds. Pop of cork. Ten seconds. Second cork. Ten seconds. Third cork. Ten seconds. Brief burst of quavering song.

KRAPP   (*sings*).   Now the day is over,
                    Night is drawing nigh-igh,
                    Shadows—

Fit of coughing. He comes back into light, sits down, wipes his mouth, switches on, resumes his listening posture.

TAPE —back on the year that is gone, with what
I hope is perhaps a glint of the old eye to
come, there is of course the house on the
canal where mother lay a-dying, in the
late autumn, after her long viduity *(Krapp
gives a start)*, and the—*(Krapp switches
off, winds back tape a little, bends his ear
closer to machine, switches on)*—a-dying,
in the late autumn, after her long viduity,
and the—

*Krapp switches off, raises his head, stares
blankly before him. His lips move in the
syllables of "viduity." No sound. He gets
up, goes backstage into darkness, comes
back with an enormous dictionary, lays it
on table, sits down and looks up the word.*

KRAPP *(reading from dictionary)*. State—or
condition of being—or remaining—a widow
—or widower. (*Looks up. Puzzled.*) Being
—or remaining? . . . (*Pause. He peers again
at dictionary. Reading.*) "Deep weeds of
viduity" . . . Also of an animal, especially
a bird . . . the vidua or weaver-bird . . .
Black plumage of male . . . (*He looks up.
With relish.*) The vidua-bird!

Pause. He closes dictionary, switches on, resumes listening posture.

TAPE —bench by the weir from where I could see her window. There I sat, in the biting wind, wishing she were gone. (*Pause.*) Hardly a soul, just a few regulars, nursemaids, infants, old men, dogs. I got to know them quite well—oh by appearance of course I mean! One dark young beauty I recollect particularly, all white and starch, incomparable bosom, with a big black hooded perambulator, most funereal thing. Whenever I looked in her direction she had her eyes on me. And yet when I was bold enough to speak to her—not having been introduced—she threatened to call a policeman. As if I had designs on her virtue! (*Laugh. Pause.*) The face she had! The eyes! Like . . . (*hesitates*) . . . chrysolite! (*Pause.*) Ah well . . . (*Pause.*) I was there when—(*Krapp switches off, broods, switches on again*)— the blind went down, one of those dirty brown roller affairs, throwing a ball for a little white dog, as chance would have it. I happened to look up and there it was. All over and done with, at last. I sat on for a few moments with the ball in my hand and the dog yelping and pawing at me. (*Pause.*) Moments. Her moments, my moments. (*Pause.*) The dog's moments. (*Pause.*) In the end I held it out to him and he took it in his mouth, gently, gently. A small, old, black, hard, solid rubber ball. (*Pause.*) I shall feel it, in my hand, until my dying day. (*Pause.*) I might have kept it. (*Pause.*) But I gave it to the dog.

Pause.

Ah well . . .

Pause.

Spiritually a year of profound gloom and indigence until that memorable night in March, at the end of the jetty, in the howling wind, never to be forgotten, when suddenly I saw the whole thing. The vision, at last. This I fancy is what I have chiefly to record this evening, against the day when my work will be done and perhaps no place left in my memory, warm or cold, for the miracle that . . . (*hesitates*) . . . for the fire that set it alight. What I suddenly saw then was this, that the belief I had been going on all my life, namely— (*Krapp switches off impatiently, winds tape forward, switches on again*)—great granite rocks the foam flying up in the light of the lighthouse and the wind-gauge spinning like a propellor, clear to me at last that the dark I have always struggled to keep under is in reality my most—(*Krapp curses, switches off, winds tape forward, switches on again*)—unshatterable association until my dissolution of storm and night with the light of the understanding and the fire—(*Krapp curses louder, switches off, winds tape forward, switches on again*)—my face in her breasts and my hand on her. We lay there without moving. But under us all moved, and moved us, gently, up and down, and from side to side.

Pause.

Past midnight. Never knew such silence. The earth might be uninhabited.

Pause.

Here I end—

Krapp switches off, winds tape back, switches on again.

—upper lake, with the punt, bathed off the bank, then pushed out into the stream and drifted. She lay stretched out on the floorboards with her hands under her head and her eyes closed. Sun blazing down, bit of a breeze, water nice and lively. I noticed a scratch on her thigh and asked her how she came by it. Picking gooseberries, she said. I said again I thought it was hopeless and no good going on, and she agreed, without opening her eyes. (*Pause.*) I asked her to look at me and after a few moments—(*pause*)—after a few moments she did, but the eyes just slits, because of the glare. I bent over her to get them in the shadow and they opened. (*Pause. Low.*) Let me in. (*Pause.*) We drifted in among

the flags and stuck. The way they went
down, sighing, before the stem! (*Pause.*)
I lay down across her with my face in her
breasts and my hand on her. We lay there
without moving. But under us all moved,
and moved us, gently, up and down, and
from side to side.

Pause.

Past midnight. Never knew—

*Krapp switches off, broods. Finally he
fumbles in his pockets, encounters the
banana, takes it out, peers at it, puts it
back, fumbles, brings out the envelope,
fumbles, puts back envelope, looks at his
watch, gets up and goes backstage into
darkness. Ten seconds. Sound of bottle
against glass, then brief siphon. Ten
seconds. Bottle against glass alone. Ten
seconds. He comes back a little unsteadily
into light, goes to front of table, takes out
keys, raises them to his eyes, chooses key.
unlocks first drawer, peers into it, feels
about inside, takes out reel, peers at it,*

locks drawer, puts keys back in his pocket, goes and sits down, takes reel off machine, lays it on dictionary, loads virgin reel on machine, takes envelope from his pocket, consults back of it, lays it on table, switches on, clears his throat and begins to record.

KRAPP   Just been listening to that stupid bastard I took myself for thirty years ago, hard to believe I was ever as bad as that. Thank God that's all done with anyway. (*Pause.*) The eyes she had! (*Broods, realizes he is recording silence, switches off, broods. Finally.*) Everything there, everything, all the—(*Realizes this is not being recorded, switches on.*) Everything there, everything on this old muckball, all the light and dark and famine and feasting of . . . (*hesitates*) . . . the ages! (*In a shout.*) Yes! (*Pause.*) Let that go! Jesus! Take his mind off his homework! Jesus! (*Pause. Weary.*) Ah well, maybe he was right. (*Pause.*) Maybe he was right. (*Broods. Realizes. Switches off. Consults envelope.*) Pah! (*Crumples it and throws it away. Broods. Switches on.*) Nothing to say, not a squeak. What's a year now? The sour cud and the iron stool. (*Pause.*) Revelled in the word spool. (*With relish.*) Spooool! Happiest moment of the past half million. (*Pause.*) Seventeen copies sold, of which eleven at trade price to free circulating libraries beyond the seas. Getting known. (*Pause.*) One pound six and something, eight I have little doubt. (*Pause.*) Crawled out once or twice, before the summer was cold. Sat shivering in the park, drowned in dreams and burning to be gone. Not a soul. (*Pause.*) Last fancies. (*Vehemently.*) Keep 'em under! (*Pause.*) Scalded the eyes out of me reading *Effie* again, a page a day, with tears again. Effie . . . (*Pause.*) Could have been happy with her, up there on the Baltic, and the pines, and the dunes. (*Pause.*) Could I? (*Pause.*) And she? (*Pause.*) Pah! (*Pause.*) Fanny came in a couple of times. Bony old ghost of a whore. Couldn't do much, but I suppose better than a kick in the crutch. The last time wasn't so bad. How do you manage it, she said, at your age? I told her I'd been saving up for her all my life. (*Pause.*) Went to Vespers once, like when I was in short trousers. (*Pause. Sings.*)

> Now the day is over,
> Night is drawing nigh-igh,
> Shadows—(*coughing, then almost inaudible*)—of the evening
> Steal across the sky.

(*Gasping.*) Went to sleep and fell off the pew. (*Pause.*) Sometimes wondered in the night if a last effort mightn't—(*Pause.*) Ah finish your booze now and get to your bed. Go on with this drivel in the morning. Or leave it at that. (*Pause.*) Leave it at that. (*Pause.*) Lie propped up in the dark —and wander. Be again in the dingle on a Christmas Eve, gathering holly, the red-berried. (*Pause.*) Be again on Croghan on a Sunday morning, in the haze, with the bitch, stop and listen to the bells. (*Pause.*) And so on. (*Pause.*) Be again, be again. (*Pause.*) All that old misery. (*Pause.*)

Once wasn't enough for you. (*Pause.*) Lie down across her.

Long pause. He suddenly bends over machine, switches off, wrenches off tape, throws it away, puts on the other, winds it forward to the passage he wants, switches on, listens staring front.

TAPE   —gooseberries, she said. I said again I thought it was hopeless and no good going on, and she agreed, without opening her eyes. (*Pause.*) I asked her to look at me and after a few moments—(*pause*)—after a few moments she did, but the eyes just slits, because of the glare. I bent over her to get them in the shadow and they opened. (*Pause. Low.*) Let me in. (*Pause.*) We drifted in among the flags and stuck. The way they went down, sighing, before the stem! (*Pause.*) I lay down across her with my face in her breasts and my hand on her. We lay there without moving. But under us all moved, and moved us, gently, up and down, and from side to side.

Pause. Krapp's lips move. No sound.

Past midnight. Never knew such silence. The earth might be uninhabited.

Pause.

Here I end this reel. Box—(*pause*)—three, spool—(*pause*)—five. (*Pause.*) Perhaps my best years are gone. When there was a chance of happiness. But I wouldn't want them back. Not with the fire in me now. No, I wouldn't want them back.

Krapp motionless staring before him. The tape runs on in silence.

CURTAIN

All
That
Fall

**A PLAY
FOR RADIO**

All That Fall was first presented by The British Broadcasting Corporation's Third Programme on January 13, 1957.

MRS. ROONEY (Maddy)   *a lady in her seventies*

CHRISTY   *a carter*

MR. TYLER   *a retired bill-broker*

MR. SLOCUM   *Clerk of the Racecourse*

TOMMY   *a porter*

MR. BARRELL   *a station-master*

MISS FITT   *a lady in her thirties*

A FEMALE VOICE

DOLLY   *a small girl*

MR. ROONEY (Dan)   *husband of Mrs. Rooney, blind*

JERRY   *a small boy*

Rural sounds. Sheep, bird, cow, cock,
severally, then together.

Silence.

Mrs. Rooney advances along country road
towards railway-station. Sound of her
dragging feet.

Music faint from house by way. "Death and
the Maiden." The steps slow down, stop.

MRS. ROONEY   Poor woman. All alone in that ruinous old
house.

Music louder. Silence but for music
playing.

The steps resume. Music dies. Mrs. Rooney
murmurs melody. Her murmur dies.

Sound of approaching cartwheels. The
cart stops. The steps slow down, stop.

MRS. ROONEY   Is that you, Christy?

CHRISTY   It is, Ma'am.

MRS. ROONEY   I thought the hinny was familiar. How is your poor wife?

CHRISTY   No better, Ma'am.

MRS. ROONEY   Your daughter then?

CHRISTY   No worse, Ma'am.

Silence.

MRS. ROONEY   Why do you halt? (*Pause.*) But why do I halt?

Silence.

CHRISTY   Nice day for the races, Ma'am.

MRS. ROONEY   No doubt it is. (*Pause.*) But will it hold up? (*Pause. With emotion.*) Will it hold up?

Silence.

CHRISTY   I suppose you wouldn't—

MRS. ROONEY   Hist! (*Pause.*) Surely to goodness that cannot be the up mail I hear already?

Silence. The hinny neighs. Silence.

CHRISTY   Damn the mail.

MRS. ROONEY   Oh thank God for that! I could have sworn I heard it, thundering up the track in the far distance. (*Pause.*) So hinnies whinny. Well, it is not surprising.

CHRISTY   I suppose you wouldn't be in need of a small load of dung?

MRS. ROONEY   Dung? What class of dung?

CHRISTY   Stydung.

MRS. ROONEY   Stydung . . . I like your frankness, Christy. (*Pause.*) I'll ask the master. (*Pause.*) Christy.

CHRISTY   Yes, Ma'am.

MRS. ROONEY   Do you find anything . . . bizarre about my way of speaking? (*Pause.*) I do not mean the voice. (*Pause.*) No, I mean the words. (*Pause. More to herself.*) I use none but the simplest words, I hope, and yet I sometimes find my way of speaking very . . . bizarre. (*Pause.*) Mercy! What was that?

CHRISTY   Never mind her, Ma'am, she's very fresh in herself to-day.
Silence.

MRS. ROONEY   Dung? What would we want with dung, at our time of life? (*Pause.*) Why are you on your feet down on the road? Why do you not climb up on the crest of your

manure and let yourself be carried along?
Is it that you have no head for heights?

Silence.

CHRISTY   (*to the hinny*). Yep! (*Pause. Louder.*) Yep
wiyya to hell owwa that!

Silence.

MRS. ROONEY   She does not move a muscle. (*Pause.*) I too
should be getting along, if I do not wish
to arrive late at the station. (*Pause.*) But a
moment ago she neighed and pawed the
ground. And now she refuses to advance.
Give her a good welt on the rump. (*Sound
of welt. Pause.*) Harder! (*Sound of welt.
Pause.*) Well! If someone were to do that
for me I should not dally. (*Pause.*) How
she gazes at me to be sure, with her great
moist cleg-tormented eyes! Perhaps if I
were to move on, down the road, out of
her field of vision . . . (*Sound of welt.*) No,
no, enough! Take her by the snaffle and
pull her eyes away from me. Oh this is
awful! (*She moves on. Sound of her
dragging feet.*) What have I done to

deserve all this, what, what? (*Dragging feet.*) So long ago . . . No! No! (*Dragging feet. Quotes.*) "Sigh out a something something tale of things, Done long ago and ill done." (*She halts.*) How can I go on, I cannot. Oh let me just flop down flat on the road like a big fat jelly out of a bowl and never move again! A great big slop thick with grit and dust and flies, they would have to scoop me up with a shovel. (*Pause.*) Heavens, there is that up mail again, what will become of me! (*The dragging steps resume.*) Oh I am just a hysterical old hag I know, destroyed with sorrow and pining and gentility and church-going and fat and rheumatism and childlessness. (*Pause. Brokenly.*) Minnie! Little Minnie! (*Pause.*) Love, that is all I asked, a little love, daily, twice daily, fifty years of twice daily love like a Paris horse-butcher's regular, what normal woman wants affection? A peck on the jaw at morning, near the ear, and another at evening, peck, peck, till you grow whiskers on you. There is that lovely laburnum again.

Dragging feet. Sound of bicycle-bell. It is old Mr. Tyler coming up behind her on his bicycle, on his way to the station. Squeak of brakes. He slows down and rides abreast of her.

MR. TYLER   Mrs. Rooney! Pardon me if I do not doff my cap, I'd fall off. Divine day for the meeting.

MRS. ROONEY   Oh, Mr. Tyler, you startled the life out of me stealing up behind me like that like a deer-stalker! Oh!

MR. TYLER   (*playfully*). I rang my bell, Mrs. Rooney, the moment I sighted you I started tinkling my bell, now don't you deny it.

MRS. ROONEY   Your bell is one thing, Mr. Tyler, and you are another. What news of your daughter?

MR. TYLER   Fair, fair. They removed everything, you know, the whole . . . er . . . bag of tricks. Now I am grandchildless.

Dragging feet.

MRS. ROONEY   Gracious how you wobble! Dismount, for mercy's sake, or ride on.

MR. TYLER   Perhaps if I were to lay my hand lightly

on your shoulder, Mrs. Rooney, how would that be? (*Pause.*) Would you permit that?

MRS. ROONEY   No, Mr. Rooney, Mr. Tyler I mean, I am tired of light old hands on my shoulders and other senseless places, sick and tired of them. Heavens, here comes Connolly's van! (*She halts. Sound of motor-van. It approaches, passes with thunderous rattle, recedes.*) Are you all right, Mr. Tyler? (*Pause.*) Where is he? (*Pause.*) Ah there you are! (*The dragging steps resume.*) That was a narrow squeak.

MR. TYLER   I alit in the nick of time.

MRS. ROONEY   It is suicide to be abroad. But what is it to be at home, Mr. Tyler, what is it to be at home? A lingering dissolution. Now we are white with dust from head to foot. I beg your pardon?

MR. TYLER   Nothing, Mrs. Rooney, nothing, I was merely cursing, under my breath, God and man, under my breath, and the wet Saturday afternoon of my conception. My back tire has gone down again. I pumped

it hard as iron before I set out. And now
I am on the rim.

MRS. ROONEY   Oh what a shame!

MR. TYLER   Now if it were the front I should not so
much mind. But the back. The back! The
chain! The oil! The grease! The hub! The
brakes! The gear! No! It is too much!
Dragging feet.

MRS. ROONEY   Are we very late, Mr. Tyler, I have not the
courage to look at my watch.

MR. TYLER   (*bitterly*). Late! I on my bicycle as I
bowled along was already late. Now
therefore we are doubly late, trebly,
quadrupedly late. Would I had shot by
you, without a word.
Dragging feet.

MRS. ROONEY   Whom are you meeting, Mr. Tyler?

MR. TYLER   Hardy. (*Pause.*) We used to climb
together. (*Pause.*) I saved his life once.
(*Pause.*) I have not forgotten it.
Dragging feet. They stop.

MRS. ROONEY   Let us a halt a moment and this vile dust

fall back upon the viler worms.
Silence. Rural sounds.

MR. TYLER   What sky! What light! Ah in spite of all it is a blessed thing to be alive in such weather, and out of hospital.

MRS. ROONEY   Alive?

MR. TYLER   Well half alive shall we say?

MRS. ROONEY   Speak for yourself, Mr. Tyler. I am not half alive nor anything approaching it. (*Pause.*) What are we standing here for? This dust will not settle in our time. And when it does some great roaring machine will come and whirl it all skyhigh again.

MR. TYLER   Well, shall we be getting along in that case?

MRS. ROONEY   No.

MR. TYLER   Come, Mrs. Rooney—

MRS. ROONEY   Go, Mr. Tyler, go on and leave me, listening to the cooing of the ringdoves. (*Cooing.*) If you see my poor blind Dan tell him I was on my way to meet him when it all came over me again, like a flood. Say to him, Your poor wife, she told

me to tell you it all came flooding over her
again and . . . (*the voice breaks*) . . . she
simply went back home . . . straight back
home . . .

MR. TYLER   Come, Mrs. Rooney, come, the mail has
not yet gone up, just take my free arm and
we'll be there with time and to spare.

MRS. ROONEY   (*sobbing*). What? What's all this now?
(*Calmer.*) Can't you see I'm in trouble?
(*With anger.*) Have you no respect for
misery? (*Sobbing.*) Minnie! Little Minnie!

MR. TYLER   Come, Mrs. Rooney, come, the mail has
not yet gone up, just take my free arm and
we'll be there with time and to spare.

MRS. ROONEY   (*brokenly*). In her forties now she'd be, I
don't know, fifty, girding up her lovely
little loins, getting ready for the change . . .

MR. TYLER   Come, Mrs. Rooney, come, the mail—

MRS. ROONEY   (*exploding*). Will you get along with you,
Mr. Rooney, Mr. Tyler I mean, will you
get along with you now and cease
molesting me? What kind of a country is
this where a woman can't weep her heart
out on the highways and byways without

being tormented by retired bill-brokers!
(*Mr. Tyler prepares to mount his bicycle.*)
Heavens, you're not going to ride her flat!
(*Mr. Tyler mounts.*) You'll tear your tube
to ribbons! (*Mr. Tyler rides off. Receding
sound of bumping bicycle. Silence.
Cooing.*) Venus birds! Billing in the woods
all the long summer long. (*Pause.*) Oh
cursed corset! If I could let it out, without
indecent exposure. Mr. Tyler! Mr. Tyler!
Come back and unlace me behind the
hedge! (*She laughs wildly, ceases.*) What's
wrong with me, what's wrong with me,
never tranquil, seething out of my dirty
old pelt, out of my skull, oh to be in atoms,
in atoms! (*Frenziedly.*) ATOMS! (*Silence.
Cooing. Faintly.*) Jesus! (*Pause.*) Jesus!

*Sound of car coming up behind her. It
slows down and draws up beside her,
engine running. It is Mr. Slocum, the Clerk
of the Racecourse.*

MR. SLOCUM   Is anything wrong, Mrs. Rooney? You are
bent all double. Have you a pain in the
stomach?

Silence. Mrs. Rooney laughs wildly.
Finally.

MRS. ROONEY   Well, if it isn't my old admirer, the Clerk of the Course, in his limousine.

MR. SLOCUM   May I offer you a lift, Mrs. Rooney? Are you going in my direction?

MRS. ROONEY   I am, Mr. Slocum, we all are. (*Pause.*) How is your poor mother?

MR. SLOCUM   Thank you, she is fairly comfortable. We manage to keep her out of pain. That is the great thing, Mrs. Rooney, is it not?

MRS. ROONEY   Yes, indeed, Mr. Slocum, that is the great thing, I don't know how you do it. (*Pause. She slaps her cheek violently.*) Ah these wasps!

MR. SLOCUM   (*coolly*). May I then offer you a seat, Madam?

MRS. ROONEY   (*with exaggerated enthusiasm*). Oh that would be heavenly, Mr. Slocum, just simply heavenly. (*Dubiously.*) But would I ever get in, you look very high off the ground to-day, these new balloon tires, I presume. (*Sound of door opening and Mrs.*

Rooney *trying to get in.*) Does this roof never come off? No? (*Efforts of Mrs. Rooney.*) No . . . I'll never do it . . . you'll have to get down, Mr. Slocum, and help me from the rear. (*Pause.*) What was that? (*Pause. Aggrieved.*) This is all your suggestion, Mr. Slocum, not mine. Drive on, Sir, drive on.

MR. SLOCUM   (*switching off the engine*). I'm coming, Mrs. Rooney, I'm coming, give me time, I'm as stiff as yourself.

Sound of Mr. Slocum extracting himself from driver's seat.

MRS. ROONEY   Stiff! Well I like that! And me heaving all over back and front. (*To herself.*) The dry old reprobate!

MR. SLOCUM   (*in position behind her*). Now, Mrs. Rooney, how shall we do this?

MRS. ROONEY   As if I were a bale, Mr. Slocum, don't be afraid. (*Pause. Sounds of effort.*) That's the way! (*Effort.*) Lower! (*Effort.*) Wait! (*Pause.*) No, don't let go! (*Pause.*) Suppose I do get up, will I ever get down?

MR. SLOCUM (*breathing hard*). You'll get down, Mrs. Rooney, you'll get down. We may not get you up, but I warrant you we'll get you down.

He resumes his efforts. Sound of these.

MRS. ROONEY Oh! . . Lower! . . Don't be afraid! . . We're past the age when . . . There! . . Now! . . Get your shoulder under it . . . Oh! . . (*Giggles.*) Oh glory! . . Up! Up! . . Ah! . . I'm in! (*Panting of Mr. Slocum. He slams the door. In a scream.*) My frock! You've nipped my frock! (*Mr. Slocum opens the door. Mrs. Rooney frees her frock. Mr. Slocum slams the door. His violent unintelligible muttering as he walks round to the other door. Tearfully.*) My nice frock! Look what you've done to my nice frock! (*Mr. Slocum gets into his seat, slams driver's door, presses starter. The engine does not start. He releases starter.*) What will Dan say when he sees me?

MR. SLOCUM Has he then recovered his sight?

MRS. ROONEY No, I mean when he knows, what will he say when he feels the hole? (*Mr. Slocum presses starter. As before. Silence.*) What are you doing, Mr. Slocum?

MR. SLOCUM   Gazing straight before me, Mrs. Rooney, through the windscreen, into the void.

MRS. ROONEY   Start her up, I beseech you, and let us be off. This is awful!

MR. SLOCUM   (*dreamily*). All morning she went like a dream and now she is dead. That is what you get for a good deed. (*Pause. Hopefully.*) Perhaps if I were to choke her. (*He does so, presses the starter. The engine roars. Roaring to make himself heard.*) She was getting too much air!

He throttles down, grinds in his first gear, moves off, changes up in a grinding of gears.

MRS. ROONEY   (*in anguish*). Mind the hen! (*Scream of brakes. Squawk of hen.*) Oh mother, you have squashed her, drive on, drive on! (*The car accelerates. Pause.*) What a death! One minute picking happy at the dung, on the road, in the sun, with now and then a dust bath, and then—bang!—all

her troubles over. (*Pause.*) All the laying
and the hatching. (*Pause.*) Just one great
squawk and then . . . peace. (*Pause.*)
They would have slit her weasand in any
case. (*Pause.*) Here we are, let me down.
(*The car slows down, stops, engine
running. Mr. Slocum blows his horn. Pause.
Louder. Pause.*) What are you up to now,
Mr. Slocum? We are at a standstill, all
danger is past and you blow your horn.
Now if instead of blowing it now you had
blown it at that unfortunate—

*Horn violently. Tommy the porter appears
at top of station steps.*

MR. SLOCUM   (*calling*). Will you come down, Tommy,
and help this lady out, she's stuck. (*Tommy
descends the steps.*) Open the door,
Tommy, and ease her out.

Tommy opens the door.

TOMMY   Certainly, Sir. Nice day for the races, Sir.
What would you fancy for—

MRS. ROONEY   Don't mind me. Don't take any notice of
me. I do not exist. The fact is well known.

MR. SLOCUM	Do as you're asked, Tommy, for the love of God.
TOMMY	Yessir. Now, Mrs. Rooney. *He starts pulling her out.*
MRS. ROONEY	Wait, Tommy, wait now, don't bustle me, just let me wheel round and get my feet to the ground. (*Her efforts to achieve this.*) Now.
TOMMY	(*pulling her out*). Mind your feather, Ma'am. (*Sounds of effort.*) Easy now, easy.
MRS. ROONEY	Wait, for God's sake, you'll have me beheaded.
TOMMY	Crouch down, Mrs. Rooney, crouch down, and get your head in the open.
MRS. ROONEY	Crouch down! At my time of life! This is lunacy!
TOMMY	Press her down, Sir. *Sounds of combined efforts.*
MRS. ROONEY	Merde!
TOMMY	Now! She's coming! Straighten up, Ma'am! There! *Mr. Slocum slams the door.*
MRS. ROONEY	Am I out?

The voice of Mr. Barrell, the station-master, raised in anger.

MR. BARRELL   Tommy! Tommy! Where the hell is he?

Mr. Slocum grinds in his gear.

TOMMY   (*hurriedly*). You wouldn't have something for the Ladies Plate, Sir, I was given Flash Harry.

MR. SLOCUM   (*scornfully*). Flash Harry! That carthorse!

MR. BARRELL   (*at top of steps, roaring*). Tommy! Blast your bleeding bloody—(*He sees Mrs. Rooney.*) Oh, Mrs. Rooney . . . (*Mr. Slocum drives away in a grinding of gears.*) Who's that crucifying his gearbox, Tommy?

TOMMY   Old Cissy Slocum.

MRS. ROONEY   Cissy Slocum! That's a nice way to refer to your betters. Cissy Slocum! And you an orphan!

MR. BARRELL   (*angrily to Tommy*). What are you doing stravaging down here on the public road? This is no place for you at all! Nip up there on the platform now and whip out the truck! Won't the twelve thirty be on top of us before we can turn round?

TOMMY (*bitterly*). And that's the thanks you get for a Christian act.

MR. BARRELL (*violently*). Get on with you now before I report you! (*Slow feet of Tommy climbing steps.*) Do you want me to come down to you with the shovel? (*The feet quicken, recede, cease.*) Ah, God forgive me, it's a hard life. (*Pause.*) Well, Mrs. Rooney, it's nice to see you up and about again. You were laid up there a long time.

MRS. ROONEY Not long enough, Mr. Barrell. (*Pause.*) Would I were still in bed, Mr. Barrell. (*Pause.*) Would I were lying stretched out in my comfortable bed, Mr. Barrell, just wasting slowly painlessly away, keeping up my strength with arrowroot and calves-foot jelly, till in the end you wouldn't see me under the blankets any more than a board. (*Pause.*) Oh no coughing or spitting or bleeding or vomiting, just drifting gently down into the higher life, and remembering, remembering . . . (*the voice breaks*) . . . all the silly unhappiness . . . as though . . . it had never happened . . . what did I do with that handkerchief? (*Sound of handkerchief loudly applied.*) How long have you been master of this station now, Mr. Barrell?

MR. BARRELL   Don't ask me, Mrs. Rooney, don't ask me.

MRS. ROONEY   You stepped into your father's shoes, I believe, when he took them off.

MR. BARRELL   Poor Pappy! (*Reverent pause.*) He didn't live long to enjoy his ease.

MRS. ROONEY   I remember him clearly. A small ferrety purple-faced widower, deaf as a doornail, very testy and snappy. (*Pause.*) I suppose you'll be retiring soon yourself, Mr. Barrell, and growing your roses. (*Pause.*) Did I understand you to say the twelve thirty would soon be upon us?

MR. BARRELL   Those were my words.

MRS. ROONEY   But according to my watch, which is more or less right—or was—by the eight o'clock news, the time is now coming up to twelve ... (*pause as she consults her watch*) ... thirty-six. (*Pause.*) And yet upon the other hand the up mail has not yet gone

through. (*Pause.*) Or has it sped by
unbeknown to me? (*Pause.*) For there was
a moment there, I remember now, I was so
plunged in sorrow I wouldn't have heard
a steam roller go over me. (*Pause. Mr.
Barrell turns to go.*) Don't go, Mr. Barrell!
(*Mr. Barrell goes. Loud.*) Mr. Barrell!
(*Pause. Louder.*) Mr. Barrell!

Mr. Barrell comes back.

MR. BARRELL   (*testily*). What is it, Mrs. Rooney, I have
my work to do.

Silence. Sound of wind.

MRS. ROONEY   The wind is getting up. (*Pause. Wind.*)
The best of the day is over. (*Pause. Wind.
Dreamily.*) Soon the rain will begin to fall
and go on falling, all afternoon. (*Mr.
Barrell goes.*) Then at evening the clouds
will part, the setting sun will shine an
instant, then sink, behind the hills. (*She
realizes Mr. Barrell has gone.*) Mr. Barrell!
Mr. Barrell! (*Silence.*) I estrange them all.
They come towards me, uninvited, bygones
bygones, full of kindness, anxious to help
. . . (*the voice breaks*) . . . genuinely

pleased . . . to see me again . . . looking so
well . . . (*Handkerchief.*) A few simple
words . . . from my heart . . . and I am all
alone . . . once more . . . (*Handkerchief.
Vehemently.*) I should not be out at all! I
should never leave the grounds! (*Pause.*)
Oh there is that Fitt woman, I wonder will
she bow to me. (*Sound of Miss Fitt
approaching, humming a hymn. She starts
climbing the steps.*) Miss Fitt! (*Miss Fitt
halts, stops humming.*) Am I then invisible,
Miss Fitt? Is this cretonne so becoming to
me that I merge into the masonry? (*Miss
Fitt descends a step.*) That is right, Miss
Fitt, look closely and you will finally
distinguish a once female shape.

MISS FITT   Mrs. Rooney! I saw you, but I did not
know you.

MRS. ROONEY   Last Sunday we worshipped together. We
knelt side by side at the same altar. We
drank from the same chalice. Have I so
changed since then?

MISS FITT   (*shocked*). Oh but in church, Mrs. Rooney,
in church I am alone with my Maker. Are

not you? (*Pause.*) Why, even the sexton
himself, you know, when he takes up the
collection, knows it is useless to pause
before me. I simply do not see the plate,
or bag, whatever it is they use, how could
I? (*Pause.*) Why even when all is over and
I go out into the sweet fresh air, why even
then for the first furlong or so I stumble in
a kind of daze as you might say, oblivious
to my coreligionists. And they are very
kind, I must admit—the vast majority—very
kind and understanding. They know me
now and take no umbrage. There she goes,
they say, there goes the dark Miss Fitt,
alone with her Maker, take no notice of
her. And they step down off the path to
avoid my running into them. (*Pause.*) Ah
yes, I am distray, very distray, even on
week-days. Ask Mother, if you do not
believe me. Hetty, she says, when I start
eating my doily instead of the thin bread
and butter, Hetty, how can you be so
distray? (*Sighs.*) I suppose the truth is I
am not there, Mrs. Rooney, just not really
there at all. I see, hear, smell, and so on, I

go through the usual motions, but my
heart is not in it, Mrs. Rooney, but heart
is in none of it. Left to myself, with no one
to check me, I would soon be flown . . .
home. (*Pause.*) So if you think I cut you
just now, Mrs. Rooney, you do me an
injustice. All I saw was a big pale blur, just
another big pale blur. (*Pause.*) Is anything
amiss, Mrs. Rooney, you do not look
normal somehow. So bowed and bent.

MRS. ROONEY   (*ruefully*). Maddy Rooney, née Dunne, the
big pale blur. (*Pause.*) You have piercing
sight, Miss Fitt, if you only knew it,
literally piercing.

Pause.

MISS FITT   Well . . . is there anything I can do, now
that I am here?

MRS. ROONEY   If you would help me up the face of this
cliff, Miss Fitt, I have little doubt your
Maker would requite you, if no one else.

MISS FITT   Now now, Mrs. Rooney, don't put your
teeth in me. Requite! I make these
sacrifices for nothing—or not at all. (*Pause.*

	Sound of her descending steps.) I take it you want to lean on me, Mrs. Rooney.
MRS. ROONEY	I asked Mr. Barrell to give me his arm, just give me his arm. (*Pause.*) He turned on his heel and strode away.
MISS FITT	Is it my arm you want then? (*Pause. Impatiently.*) Is it my arm you want, Mrs. Rooney, or what is it?
MRS. ROONEY	(*exploding*). Your arm! Any arm! A helping hand! For five seconds! Christ, what a planet!
MISS FITT	Really . . . Do you know what it is, Mrs. Rooney, I do not think it is wise of you to be going about at all.
MRS. ROONEY	(*violently*). Come down here, Miss Fitt, and give me your arm, before I scream down the parish!
	Pause. Wind. Sound of Miss Fitt descending last steps.
MISS FITT	(*resignedly*). Well, I suppose it is the Protestant thing to do.
MRS. ROONEY	Pismires do it for one another. (*Pause.*) I have seen slugs do it. (*Miss Fitt proffers*

her arm.) No, the other side, my dear, if it's all the same to you, I'm left-handed on top of everything else. (*She takes Miss Fitt's right arm.*) Heavens, child, you're just a bag of bones, you need building up. (*Sound of her toiling up steps on Miss Fitt's arm.*) This is worse than the Matterhorn, were you ever up the Matterhorn, Miss Fitt, great honeymoon resort. (*Sound of toiling.*) Why don't they have a handrail? (*Panting.*) Wait till I get some air. (*Pause.*) Don't let me go! (*Miss Fitt hums her hymn. After a moment Mrs. Rooney joins in with the words.*) . . . the encircling gloo-oom (*Miss Fitt stops humming*) . . . tum tum me on. (*Forte.*) The night is dark and I am far from ho-ome, tum tum—

MISS FITT (*hysterically*). Stop it, Mrs. Rooney, stop it, or I'll drop you!

MRS. ROONEY Wasn't it that they sung on the Lusitania? Or Rock of Ages? Most touching it must have been. Or was it the Titanic?

Attracted by the noise a group, including Mr. Tyler, Mr. Barrell and Tommy, gathers at top of steps.

MR. BARRELL   What the—

Silence.

MR. TYLER   Lovely day for the fixture.

*Loud titter from Tommy cut short by Mr.
Barrell with backhanded blow in the
stomach. Appropriate noise from Tommy.*

FEMALE VOICE   (*shrill*). Oh look, Dolly, look!

DOLLY   What, Mamma?

FEMALE VOICE   They are stuck! (*Cackling laugh.*) They
are stuck!

MRS. ROONEY   Now we are the laughing-stock of the
twenty-six counties. Or is it thirty-six?

MR. TYLER   That is a nice way to treat your defenceless
subordinates, Mr. Barrell, hitting them
without warning in the pit of the stomach.

MISS FITT   Has anybody seen my mother?

MR. BARRELL   Who is that?

TOMMY   The dark Miss Fitt.

MR. BARRELL   Where is her face?

MRS. ROONEY   Now, deary, I am ready if you are. (*They toil up remaining steps.*) Stand back, you cads!

Shuffle of feet.

FEMALE VOICE   Mind yourself, Dolly!

MRS. ROONEY   Thank you, Miss Fitt, thank you, that will do, just prop me up against the wall like a roll of tarpaulin and that will be all, for the moment. (*Pause.*) I am sorry for all this ramdam, Miss Fitt, had I known you were looking for your mother I should not have importuned you, I know what it is.

MR. TYLER   (*in marvelling aside*). Ramdam!

FEMALE VOICE   Come, Dolly darling, let us take up our stand before the first-class smokers. Give me your hand and hold me tight, one can be sucked under.

MR. TYLER   You have lost your mother, Miss Fitt?

MISS FITT   Good-morning, Mr. Tyler.

MR. TYLER   Good-morning, Miss Fitt.

MR. BARRELL   Good-morning, Miss Fitt.

MISS FITT   Good-morning, Mr. Barrell.

MR. TYLER   You have lost your mother, Miss Fitt?

MISS FITT   She said she would be on the last train.

MRS. ROONEY   Do not imagine, because I am silent, that I am not present, and alive, to all that is going on.

MR. TYLER   (*to Miss Fitt*). When you say the last train—

MRS. ROONEY   Do not flatter yourselves for one moment, because I hold aloof, that my sufferings have ceased. No. The entire scene, the hills, the plain, the racecourse with its miles and miles of white rails and three red stands, the pretty little wayside station, even you yourselves, yes, I mean it, and over all the clouding blue, I see it all, I stand here and see it all with eyes . . . (*the voice breaks.*) . . . through eyes . . . oh, if you had my eyes . . . you would understand . . . the things they have seen . . . and not looked away . . . this is nothing . . . nothing . . . what did I do with that handkerchief?

Pause.

MR. TYLER (*to Miss Fitt*). When you say the last train—(*Mrs. Rooney blows her nose violently and long*)—when you say the last train, Miss Fitt, I take it you mean the twelve thirty.

MISS FITT What else could I mean, Mr. Tyler, what else could I *conceivably* mean?

MR. TYLER Then you have no cause for anxiety, Miss Fitt, for the twelve thirty has not yet arrived. Look. (*Miss Fitt looks.*) No, up the line. (*Miss Fitt looks. Patiently.*) No, Miss Fitt, follow the direction of my index. (*Miss Fitt looks.*) There. You see now. The signal. At the bawdy hour of nine. (*In rueful afterthought.*) Or three alas! (*Mr. Barrell stifles a guffaw.*) Thank you, Mr. Barrell.

MISS FITT But the time is now getting on for—

MR. TYLER (*patiently*). We all know, Miss Fitt, we all know only too well what the time is now getting on for, and yet the cruel fact remains that the twelve thirty has not yet arrived.

MISS FITT Not an accident, I trust! (*Pause.*) Do not

tell me she has left the track! (*Pause.*) Oh darling mother! With the fresh sole for lunch!

Loud titter from Tommy, checked as before by Mr. Barrell.

MR. BARRELL   That's enough old guff out of you. Nip up to the box now and see has Mr. Case anything for me.

Tommy goes.

MRS. ROONEY   (*sadly*). Poor Dan!

MISS FITT   (*in anguish*). What terrible thing has happened?

MR. TYLER   Now now, Miss Fitt, do not—

MRS. ROONEY   (*with vehement sadness*). Poor Dan!

MR. TYLER   Now now, Miss Fitt, do not give way . . . to despair, all will come right . . . in the end. (*Aside to Mr. Barrell.*) What *is* the situation, Mr. Barrell? Not a collision surely?

MRS. ROONEY   (*enthusiastically*). A collision! Oh that would be wonderful!

MISS FITT   (*horrified*). A collision! I knew it!

MR. TYLER   Come, Miss Fitt, let us move a little up the platform.

MRS. ROONEY   Yes, let us all do that. (*Pause.*) No? (*Pause.*) You have changed your mind? (*Pause.*) I quite agree, we are better here, in the shadow of the waiting-room.

MR. BARRELL   Excuse me a moment.

MRS. ROONEY   Before you slink away, Mr. Barrell, please, a statement of some kind, I insist. Even the slowest train on this brief line is not ten minutes and more behind its scheduled time without good cause, one imagines. (*Pause.*) We all know your station is the best kept of the entire network, but there are times when that is not enough, just not enough. (*Pause.*) Now, Mr. Barrell, leave off chewing your whiskers, we are waiting to hear from you—we the unfortunate ticket-holders' nearest if not dearest.

    Pause.

MR. TYLER   (*reasonably*). I do think we are owed some kind of explanation, Mr. Barrell, if only to set our minds at rest.

MR. BARRELL   I know nothing. All I know is there has been a hitch. All traffic is retarded.

MRS. ROONEY   (*derisively*). Retarded! A hitch! Ah these celibates! Here we are eating our hearts out with anxiety for our loved ones and he calls that a hitch! Those of us like myself with heart and kidney trouble may collapse at any moment and he calls that a hitch! In our ovens the Saturday roast is burning to a shrivel and he calls that—

MR. TYLER   Here comes Tommy, running! I am glad I have been spared to see this.

TOMMY   (*excitedly, in the distance*). She's coming. (*Pause. Nearer.*) She's at the level-crossing!

Immediately exaggerated station sounds. Falling signals. Bells. Whistles. Crescendo of train whistle approaching. Sound of train rushing through station.

MRS. ROONEY   (*above rush of train*). The up mail! The up mail! (*The up mail recedes, the down train approaches, enters the station, pulls up with great hissing of steam and clashing of couplings. Noise of passengers descending, doors banging, Mr. Barrell shouting "Boghill! Boghill!", etc. Piercingly.*) Dan! . . Are you all right? . . Where is he? . . Dan! . . Did you see my husband? . . Dan! . . (*Noise of station emptying. Guard's whistle. Train departing, receding. Silence.*) He isn't on it! The misery I have endured, to get here, and he isn't on it! . . Mr. Barrell! . . Was he not on it? (*Pause.*) Is anything the matter, you look as if you had seen a ghost. (*Pause.*) Tommy! . . Did you see the master?

TOMMY   He'll be along, Ma'am, Jerry is minding him.

Mr. Rooney suddenly appears on platform, advancing on small boy Jerry's arm. He is blind, thumps the ground with his stick and pants incessantly.

MRS. ROONEY   Oh, Dan! There you are! (*Her dragging feet as she hastens towards him. She reaches him. They halt.*) Where in the world were you?

MR. ROONEY   (*coolly.*) Maddy.

MRS. ROONEY	Where were you all this time?
MR. ROONEY	In the men's.
MRS. ROONEY	Kiss me!
MR. ROONEY	Kiss you? In public? On the platform? Before the boy? Have you taken leave of your senses?
MRS. ROONEY	Jerry wouldn't mind. Would you, Jerry?
JERRY	No, Ma'am.
MRS. ROONEY	How is your poor father?
JERRY	They took him away, Ma'am.
MRS. ROONEY	Then you are all alone?
JERRY	Yes, Ma'am.
MR. ROONEY	Why are you here? You did not notify me
MRS. ROONEY	I wanted to give you a surprise. For your birthday.
MR. ROONEY	My birthday?
MRS. ROONEY	Don't you remember? I wished you your happy returns in the bathroom.
MR. ROONEY	I did not hear you.
MRS. ROONEY	But I gave you a tie! You have it on! *Pause.*

MR. ROONEY   How old am I now?

MRS. ROONEY   Now never mind about that. Come.

MR. ROONEY   Why did you not cancel the boy? Now we shall have to give him a penny.

MRS. ROONEY   (*miserably*). I forgot! I had such a time getting here! Such horrid nasty people! (*Pause. Pleading.*) Be nice to me, Dan, be nice to me today!

MR. ROONEY   Give the boy a penny.

MRS. ROONEY   Here are two halfpennies, Jerry. Run along now and buy yourself a nice gobstopper.

JERRY   Yes, Ma'am.

MR. ROONEY   Come for me on Monday, if I am still alive.

JERRY   Yessir.

He runs off.

MR. ROONEY   We could have saved sixpence. We have saved fivepence. (*Pause.*) But at what cost?

They move off along platform arm in arm. Dragging feet, panting, thudding stick.

MRS. ROONEY   Are you not well?

They halt, on Mr. Rooney's initiative.

MR. ROONEY   Once and for all, do not ask me to speak
                and move at the same time. I shall not say
                this in this life again.

                *They move off. Dragging feet, etc. They
                halt at top of steps.*

MRS. ROONEY   Are you not—

MR. ROONEY   Let us get this precipice over.

MRS. ROONEY   Put your arm round me.

MR. ROONEY   Have you been drinking again? (*Pause.*)
                You are quivering like a blanc-mange.
                (*Pause.*) Are you in a condition to lead
                me? (*Pause.*) We shall fall into the ditch.

MRS. ROONEY   Oh, Dan! It will be like old times!

MR. ROONEY   Pull yourself together or I shall send
                Tommy for the cab. Then, instead of
                having saved sixpence, no, fivepence, we
                shall have lost . . . (*calculating mumble*)
                . . . two and three less six one and no plus
                one one and no plus three one and nine
                and one ten and three two and one . . .
                (*normal voice*) two and one, we shall be
                the poorer to the tune of two and one.
                (*Pause.*) Curse that sun, it has gone in.

What is the day doing?

Wind.

MRS. ROONEY   Shrouding, shrouding, the best of it is past.
(*Pause.*) Soon the first great drops will
fall splashing in the dust.

MR. ROONEY   And yet the glass was firm. (*Pause.*) Let us
hasten home and sit before the fire. We
shall draw the blinds. You will read to me.
I think Effie is going to commit adultery
with the Major. (*Brief drag of feet.*) Wait!
(*Feet cease. Stick tapping at steps.*) I have
been up and down these steps five
thousand times and still I do not know how
many there are. When I think there are
six there are four or five or seven or eight
and when I remember there are five there
are three or four or six or seven and when
finally I realize there are seven there are
five or six or eight or nine. Sometimes I
wonder if they do not change them in the
night. (*Pause. Irritably.*) Well? How many
do you make them to-day?

MRS. ROONEY   Do not ask me to count, Dan, not now.

MR. ROONEY	Not count! One of the few satisfactions in life?
MRS. ROONEY	Not steps, Dan, please, I always get them wrong. Then you might fall on your wound and I would have that on my manure-heap on top of everything else. No, just cling to me and all will be well.
	Confused noise of their descent. Panting, stumbling, ejaculations, curses. Silence.
MR. ROONEY	Well! That is what you call well!
MRS. ROONEY	We are down. And little the worse. (*Silence. A donkey brays. Silence.*) That was a true donkey. Its father and mother were donkeys.
	Silence.
MR. ROONEY	Do you know what it is, I think I shall retire.
MRS. ROONEY	(*appalled*). Retire! And live at home? On your grant!
MR. ROONEY	Never tread these cursed steps again. Trudge this hellish road for the last time. Sit at home on the remnants of my bottom

counting the hours—till the next meal. (*Pause.*) The very thought puts life in me! Forward, before it dies!

They move on. Dragging feet, panting, thudding stick.

MRS. ROONEY   Now mind, here is the path . . . Up! . . Well done! Now we are in safety and a straight run home.

MR. ROONEY   (*without halting, between gasps*). A straight . . . run! . . She calls that . . . a straight . . . run! . .

MRS. ROONEY   Hush! do not speak as you go along, you know it is not good for your coronary. (*Dragging steps, etc.*) Just concentrate on putting one foot before the next or whatever the expression is. (*Dragging feet, etc.*) That is the way, now we are doing nicely. (*Dragging feet, etc. They suddenly halt, on Mrs. Rooney's initiative.*) Heavens! I knew there was something! With all the excitement! I forgot!

MR. ROONEY   (*quietly*). Good God.

MRS. ROONEY   But you must know, Dan, of course, you

	were on it. What ever happened? Tell me!
MR. ROONEY	I have never known anything to happen.
MRS. ROONEY	But you must—
MR. ROONEY	(*violently*). All this stopping and starting again is devilish, devilish! I get a little way on me and begin to be carried along when suddenly you stop dead! Two hundred pounds of unhealthy fat! What possessed you to come out at all? Let go of me!
MRS. ROONEY	(*in great agitation*). No, I must know, we won't stir from here till you tell me. Fifteen minutes late! On a thirty minute run! It's unheard of!
MR. ROONEY	I know nothing. Let go of me before I shake you off.
MRS. ROONEY	But you must know! You were on it! Was it at the terminus? Did you leave on time? Or was it on the line? (*Pause.*) Did something happen on the line? (*Pause.*) Dan! (*Brokenly.*) Why won't you tell me!
	Silence. They move off. Dragging feet, etc. They halt. Pause.
MR. ROONEY	Poor Maddy! (*Pause. Children's cries.*)

What was that?

Pause for Mrs. Rooney to ascertain.

MRS. ROONEY   The Lynch twins jeering at us.

Cries.

MR. ROONEY   Will they pelt us with mud to-day, do you suppose?

Cries.

MRS. ROONEY   Let us turn and face them. (*Cries. They turn. Silence.*) Threaten them with your stick. (*Silence.*) They have run away.

Pause.

MR. ROONEY   Did you ever wish to kill a child? (*Pause.*) Nip some young doom in the bud. (*Pause.*) Many a time at night, in winter, on the black road home, I nearly attacked the boy. (*Pause.*) Poor Jerry! (*Pause.*) What restrained me then? (*Pause.*) Not fear of man. (*Pause.*) Shall we go on backwards now a little?

MRS. ROONEY   Backwards?

MR. ROONEY   Yes. Or you forwards and I backwards. The perfect pair. Like Dante's damned,

with their faces arsy-versy. Our tears will
water our bottoms.

MRS. ROONEY   What is the matter, Dan? Are you not
well?

MR. ROONEY   Well! Did you ever know me to be well?
The day you met me I should have been
in bed. The day you proposed to me the
doctors gave me up. You knew that, did
you not? The night you married me they
came for me with an ambulance. You have
not forgotten that, I suppose? (*Pause*.)
No, I cannot be said to be well. But I am
no worse. Indeed I am better than I was.
The loss of my sight was a great fillip. If I
could go deaf and dumb I think I might
pant on to be a hundred. Or have I done
so? (*Pause*.) Was I a hundred to-day?
(*Pause*.) Am I a hundred, Maddy?
Silence.

MRS. ROONEY   All is still. No living soul in sight. There is
no one to ask. The world is feeding. The
wind—(*brief wind*)—scarcely stirs the
leaves and the birds—(*brief chirp*)—are
tired singing. The cows—(*brief moo*)—and

sheep—(*brief baa*)—ruminate in silence. The dogs—(*brief bark*)—are hushed and the hens—(*brief cackle*)—sprawl torpid in the dust. We are alone. There is no one to ask.

Silence.

MR. ROONEY   (*clearing his throat, narrative tone*). We drew out on the tick of time, I can vouch for that. I was—

MRS. ROONEY   How can you vouch for it?

MR. ROONEY   (*normal tone, angrily*). I can vouch for it, I tell you! Do you want my relation or don't you? (*Pause. Narrative tone.*) On the tick of time. I had the compartment to myself, as usual. At least I hope so, for I made no attempt to restrain myself. My mind—(*Normal tone.*) But why do we not sit down somewhere? Are we afraid we should never rise again?

MRS. ROONEY   Sit down on what?

MR. ROONEY   On a bench, for example.

MRS. ROONEY   There is no bench.

MR. ROONEY   Then on a bank, let us sink down upon a bank.

MRS. ROONEY   There is no bank.

MR. ROONEY   Then we cannot. (*Pause.*) I dream of other roads, in other lands. Of another home, another—(*he hesitates*)—another home. (*Pause.*) What was I trying to say?

MRS. ROONEY   Something about your mind.

MR. ROONEY   (*startled*). My mind? Are you sure. (*Pause. Incredulous.*) My mind? . . (*Pause.*) Ah yes. (*Narrative tone.*) Alone in the compartment my mind began to work, as so often after office hours, on the way home, in the train, to the lilt of the bogeys. Your season-ticket, I said, costs you twelve pounds a year and you earn, on an average, seven and six a day, that is to say barely enough to keep you alive and twitching with the help of food, drink, tobacco and periodicals until you finally reach home and fall into bed. Add to this—or subtract from it—rent, stationery, various subscriptions, tramfares to and fro, light and heat, permits and licences, hairtrims and shaves, tips to escorts, upkeep of premises and appearances, and a thousand unspecifiable sundries, and it is clear that by lying at home in bed, day and night, winter and summer, with a change of pyjamas once a fortnight, you would add very considerably to your income. Business, I said—(*A cry. Pause. Again. Normal tone.*) Did I hear a cry?

MRS. ROONEY Mrs. Tully, I fancy. Her poor husband is in constant pain and beats her unmercifully.

Silence.

MR. ROONEY That was a short knock. (*Pause.*) What was I trying to get at?

MRS. ROONEY Business.

MR. ROONEY Ah yes, business. (*Narrative tone.*) Business, old man, I said, retire from business, it has retired from you. (*Normal tone.*) One has these moments of lucidity.

MRS. ROONEY I feel very cold and weak.

MR. ROONEY (*narrative tone*). On the other hand, I said, there are the horrors of home life, the dusting, sweeping, airing, scrubbing, waxing, waning, washing, mangling, drying, mowing, clipping, raking, rolling, scuffling, shovelling, grinding, tearing, pounding, banging and slamming. And the brats, the happy little hearty little howling neighbours' brats. Of all this and much more the week-end, the Saturday intermission and then the day of rest, have given you some idea. But what must it be like on a working-day? A Wednesday? A Friday! What must it be like on a Friday! And I fell to thinking of my silent, backstreet, basement office, with its obliterated plate, rest-couch and velvet hangings, and what it means to be buried there alive, if only from ten to five, with convenient to the one hand a bottle of light pale ale and to the other a long ice-cold fillet of hake. Nothing, I said, not even fully certified death, can ever take the place of that. It was then I noticed we were at a standstill. (*Pause. Normal tone. Irritably.*) Why are you hanging out of me like that? Have you swooned away?

MRS. ROONEY   I feel very cold and faint. The wind—

(*whistling wind*)—is whistling through my summer frock as if I had nothing on over my bloomers. I have had no solid food since my elevenses.

MR. ROONEY   You have ceased to care. I speak—and you listen to the wind.

MRS. ROONEY   No no, I am agog, tell me all, then we shall press on and never pause, never pause, till we come safe to haven.

Pause.

MR. ROONEY   Never pause . . . safe to haven . . . Do you know, Maddy, sometimes one would think you were struggling with a dead language.

MRS. ROONEY   Yes indeed, Dan, I know full well what you mean, I often have that feeling, it is unspeakably excruciating.

MR. ROONEY   I confess I have it sometimes myself, when I happen to overhear what I am saying.

MRS. ROONEY   Well, you know, it will be dead in time, just like our own poor dear Gaelic, there is that to be said.

Urgent baa.

MR. ROONEY   (*startled*). Good God!

MRS. ROONEY   Oh, the pretty little woolly lamb, crying to suck its mother! Theirs has not changed, since Arcady.

Pause.

MR. ROONEY   Where was I in my composition?

MRS. ROONEY   At a standstill.

MR. ROONEY   Ah yes. (*Clears his throat. Narrative tone.*) I concluded naturally that we had entered a station and would soon be on our way again, and I sat on, without misgiving. Not a sound. Things are very dull to-day, I said, nobody getting down, nobody getting on. Then as time flew by and nothing happened I realized my error. We had not entered a station.

MRS. ROONEY   Did you not spring up and poke your head out of the window?

MR. ROONEY   What good would that have done me?

MRS. ROONEY   Why to call out to be told what was amiss.

MR. ROONEY   I did not care what was amiss. No, I just sat on, saying, If this train were never to move again I should not greatly mind.

Then gradually a—how shall I say—a growing desire to—er—you know—welled up within me. Nervous probably. In fact now I am sure. You know, the feeling of being confined.

MRS. ROONEY Yes yes, I have been through that.

MR. ROONEY If we sit here much longer, I said, I really do not know what I shall do. I got up and paced to and fro between the seats, like a caged beast.

MRS. ROONEY That is a help sometimes.

MR. ROONEY After what seemed an eternity we simply moved off. And the next thing was Barrell bawling the abhorred name. I got down and Jerry led me to the men's, or Fir as they call it now, from Vir Viris I suppose, the *V* becoming *F*, in accordance with Grimm's Law. (*Pause.*) The rest you know. (*Pause.*) You say nothing? (*Pause.*) Say something, Maddy. Say you believe me.

MRS. ROONEY I remember once attending a lecture by one of these new mind doctors, I forget what you call them. He spoke—

MR. ROONEY   A lunatic specialist?

MRS. ROONEY   No no, just the troubled mind, I was hoping he might shed a little light on my lifelong preoccupation with horses' buttocks.

MR. ROONEY   A neurologist.

MRS. ROONEY   No no, just mental distress, the name will come back to me in the night. I remember his telling us the story of a little girl, very strange and unhappy in her ways, and how he treated her unsuccessfully over a period of years and was finally obliged to give up the case. He could find nothing wrong with her, he said. The only thing wrong with her as far as he could see was that she was dying. And she did in fact die, shortly after he washed his hands of her.

MR. ROONEY   Well? What is there so wonderful about that?

MRS. ROONEY   No, it was just something he said, and the way he said it, that have haunted me ever since.

MR. ROONEY   You lie awake at night, tossing to and fro and brooding on it.

MRS. ROONEY   On it and other . . . wretchedness. (*Pause.*) When he had done with the little girl he stood there motionless for some time, quite two minutes I should say, looking down at his table. Then he suddenly raised his head and exclaimed, as if he had had a revelation, The trouble with her was she had never been really born! (*Pause.*) He spoke throughout without notes. (*Pause.*) I left before the end.

MR. ROONEY   Nothing about your buttocks? (*Mrs. Rooney weeps. In affectionate remonstrance.*) Maddy!

MRS. ROONEY   There is nothing to be done for those people!

MR. ROONEY   For which is there? (*Pause.*) That does not sound right somehow. (*Pause.*) What way am I facing?

MRS. ROONEY   What?

MR. ROONEY   I have forgotten what way I am facing.

MRS. ROONEY   You have turned aside and are bowed

down over the ditch.

MR. ROONEY   There is a dead dog down there.

MRS. ROONEY   No no, just the rotting leaves.

MR. ROONEY   In June? Rotting leaves in June?

MRS. ROONEY   Yes dear, from last year, and from the year before last, and from the year before that again. (*Silence. Rainy wind. They move on. Dragging steps, etc.*) There is that lovely laburnum again. Poor thing, it is losing all its tassels. (*Dragging steps, etc.*) There are the first drops. (*Rain. Dragging feet, etc.*) Golden drizzle. (*Dragging steps, etc.*) Do not mind me, dear, I am just talking to myself. (*Rain heavier. Dragging steps, etc.*) Can hinnies procreate, I wonder.

They halt, on Mr. Rooney's initiative.

MR. ROONEY   Say that again.

MRS. ROONEY   Come on, dear, don't mind me, we are getting drenched.

MR. ROONEY   (*forcibly*). Can what what?

MRS. ROONEY   Hinnies procreate. (*Silence.*) You know,

hinnies, or is it jinnies, aren't they barren, or sterile, or whatever it is? (*Pause.*) It wasn't an ass's colt at all, you know, I asked the Regius Professor.

Pause.

MR. ROONEY He should know.

MRS. ROONEY Yes, it was a hinny, he rode into Jerusalem or wherever it was on a hinny. (*Pause.*) That must mean something. (*Pause.*) It's like the sparrows, than many of which we are of more value, they weren't sparrows at all.

MR. ROONEY Than many of which . . . You exaggerate, Maddy.

MRS. ROONEY (*with emotion*). They weren't sparrows at all!

MR. ROONEY Does that put our price up?

Silence. They move on. Wind and rain. Dragging feet, etc. They halt.

MRS. ROONEY Do you want some dung? (*Silence. They move on. Wind and rain, etc. They halt.*) Why do you stop? Do you want to say something?

MR. ROONEY   No.

MRS. ROONEY   Then why do you stop?

MR. ROONEY   It is easier.

MRS. ROONEY   Are you very wet?

MR. ROONEY   To the buff.

MRS. ROONEY   The buff?

MR. ROONEY   The buff. From buffalo.

MRS. ROONEY   We shall hang up all our things in the hot-cupboard and get into our dressing-gowns. (*Pause.*) Put your arm round me. (*Pause.*) Be nice to me! (*Pause. Gratefully.*) Ah Dan! (*They move on. Wind and rain. Dragging feet, etc. Faintly same music as before. They halt. Music clearer. Silence but for music playing. Music dies.*) All day the same old record. All alone in that great empty house. She must be a very old woman now.

MR. ROONEY   (*indistinctly*). Death and the Maiden.

Silence.

MRS. ROONEY   You are crying. (*Pause.*) Are you crying?

MR. ROONEY   (*violently*). Yes! (*They move on. Wind*

and rain. Dragging feet, etc. They halt.
They move on. Wind and rain. Dragging
feet, etc. They halt.) Who is the preacher
to-morrow? The incumbent?

MRS. ROONEY   No.

MR. ROONEY   Thank God for that. Who?

MRS. ROONEY   Hardy.

MR. ROONEY   "How to be Happy though Married"?

MRS. ROONEY   No no, he died, you remember. No connexion.

MR. ROONEY   Has he announced the text?

MRS. ROONEY   "The Lord upholdeth all that fall and
raiseth up all those that be bowed down."
(*Silence. They join in wild laughter. They*
move on. Wind and rain. Dragging feet,
etc.) Hold me tighter, Dan! (*Pause.*) Oh
yes!

They halt.

MR. ROONEY   I hear something behind us.

Pause.

MRS. ROONEY   It looks like Jerry. (*Pause.*) It is Jerry.

Sound of Jerry's running steps approach-

ing. He halts beside them, panting.

JERRY (*panting*). You dropped—

MRS. ROONEY Take your time, my little man, you will burst a bloodvessel.

JERRY (*panting*). You dropped something, Sir, Mr. Barrell told me to run after you.

MRS. ROONEY Show. (*She takes the object.*) What is it? (*She examines it.*) What is this thing, Dan?

MR. ROONEY Perhaps it is not mine at all.

JERRY Mr. Barrell said it was, Sir.

MRS. ROONEY It looks like a kind of ball. And yet it is not a ball.

MR. ROONEY Give it to me.

MRS. ROONEY (*giving it*). What *is* it, Dan?

MR. ROONEY It is a thing I carry about with me.

MRS. ROONEY Yes, but what—

MR. ROONEY (*violently*). It is a thing I carry about with me!

Silence. Mrs. Rooney looks for a penny.

MRS. ROONEY I have no small money. Have you?

MR. ROONEY	I have none of any kind.
MRS. ROONEY	We are out of change, Jerry. Remind Mr. Rooney on Monday and he will give you a penny for your pains.
JERRY	Yes, Ma'am.
MR. ROONEY	If I am alive.
JERRY	Yessir.

Jerry starts running back towards the station.

MRS. ROONEY	Jerry! (*Jerry halts.*) Did you hear what the hitch was? (*Pause.*) Did you hear what kept the train so late?
MR. ROONEY	How would he have heard? Come on.
MRS. ROONEY	What was it, Jerry?
JERRY	It was a—
MR. ROONEY	Leave the boy alone, he knows nothing! Come on!
MRS. ROONEY	What was it, Jerry?
JERRY	It was a little child, Ma'am.

Mr. Rooney groans.

MRS. ROONEY	What do you mean, it was a little child?
JERRY	It was a little child fell out of the carriage,

On to the line, Ma'am. (*Pause.*) Under
the wheels, Ma'am.

*Silence. Jerry runs off. His steps die away.
Tempest of wind and rain. It abates. They
move on. Dragging steps, etc. They halt.
Tempest of wind and rain.*

Embers

A PLAY
FOR RADIO

Embers was first produced by The British Broadcasting Corporation's Third Programme on June 24, 1959.

Sea scarcely audible.
HENRY's *boots on shingle. He halts.*
Sea a little louder.

HENRY   On. (*Sea. Voice louder.*) On! (*He moves
on. Boots on shingle. As he goes.*) Stop.
(*Boots on shingle. As he goes, louder.*)
Stop! (*He halts. Sea a little louder.*) Down.
(*Sea. Voice louder.*) Down! (*Slither of
shingle as he sits. Sea, still faint, audible
throughout what follows whenever pause
indicated.*) Who is beside me now?
(*Pause.*) An old man, blind and foolish.
(*Pause.*) My father, back from the dead,
to be with me. (*Pause.*) As if he hadn't
died. (*Pause.*) No, simply back from the
dead to be with me, in this strange place.
(*Pause.*) Can he hear me? (*Pause.*) Yes,
he must hear me. (*Pause.*) To answer me?
(*Pause.*) No, he doesn't answer me.
(*Pause.*) Just to be with me. (*Pause.*) That
sound you hear is the sea. (*Pause.
Louder.*) I say that sound you hear is the

sea, we are sitting on the strand. (*Pause.*)
I mention it because the sound is so
strange, so unlike the sound of the sea,
that if you didn't see what it was you
wouldn't know what it was. (*Pause.*)
Hooves! (*Pause. Louder.*) Hooves! (*Sound
of hooves walking on hard road. They die
rapidly away. Pause.*) Again! (*Hooves as
before. Pause. Excitedly.*) Train it to mark
time! Shoe it with steel and tie it up in the
yard, have it stamp all day! (*Pause.*) A ten
ton mammoth back from the dead, shoe it
with steel and have it tramp the world
down! (*Pause.*) Listen to it! (*Pause.*)
Listen to the light now, you always loved
light, not long past noon and all the shore
in shadow and the sea out as far as the
island. (*Pause.*) You would never live this
side of the bay, you wanted the sun on the
water for that evening bathe you took once
too often. But when I got your money I
moved across, as perhaps you may know.
(*Pause.*) We never found your body, you
know, that held up probate an unconscion-
able time, they said there was nothing to

prove you hadn't run away from us all and
alive and well under a false name in the
Argentine for example, that grieved
mother greatly. (*Pause.*) I'm like you in
that, can't stay away from it, but I never
go in, no, I think the last time I went in was
with you. (*Pause.*) Just be near it.
(*Pause.*) Today it's calm, but I often hear
it above in the house and walking the roads
and start talking, oh just loud enough to
drown it, nobody notices. (*Pause.*) But I'd
be talking now no matter where I was, I
once went to Switzerland to get away from
the cursed thing and never stopped all the
time I was there. (*Pause.*) I usen't to need
anyone, just to myself, stories, there was a
great one about an old fellow called
Bolton, I never finished it, I never finished
anything, everything always went on for
ever. (*Pause.*) Bolton. (*Pause. Louder.*)
Bolton! (*Pause.*) There before the fire.
(*Pause.*) Before the fire with all the
shutters . . . no, hangings, hangings, all
the hangings drawn and the light, no light,
only the light of the fire, sitting there in the

... no, standing, standing there on the
hearthrug in the dark before the fire with
his arms on the chimney-piece and his
head on his arms, standing there waiting in
the dark before the fire in his old red
dressing-gown and no sound in the house
of any kind, only the sound of the fire.
(*Pause.*) Standing there in his old red
dressing-gown might go on fire any minute
like when he was a child, no, that was his
pyjamas, standing there waiting in the
dark, no light, only the light of the fire,
and no sound of any kind, only the fire, an
old man in great trouble. (*Pause.*) Ring
then at the door and over he goes to the
window and looks out between the
hangings, fine old chap, very big and
strong, bright winter's night, snow
everywhere, bitter cold, white world, cedar
boughs bending under load, and then as
the arm goes up to ring again recognizes
... Holloway ... (*long pause*) ... yes,
Holloway, recognizes Holloway, goes
down and opens. (*Pause.*) Outside all still,
not a sound, dog's chain maybe or a bough

groaning if you stood there listening long
enough, white world, Holloway with his
little black bag, not a sound, bitter cold,
full moon small and white, crooked trail of
Holloway's galoshes. Vega in the Lyre very
green. (*Pause.*) Vega in the Lyre very
green. (*Pause.*) Following conversation
then on the step, no, in the room, back in
the room, following conversation then back
in the room, Holloway: "My dear Bolton,
it is now past midnight, if you would be
good enough—", gets no further, Bolton:
"Please! PLEASE!" Dead silence then, not
a sound, only the fire, all coal, burning
down now. Holloway on the hearthrug
trying to toast his arse, Bolton, where's
Bolton, no light, only the fire, Bolton at the
window, his back to the hangings, holding
them a little apart with his hand, looking
out, white world, even the spire, white to
the vane, most unusual, silence in the
house, not a sound, only the fire, no flames
now, embers. (*Pause.*) Embers. (*Pause.*)
Shifting, lapsing, furtive like, dreadful
sound, Holloway on the rug, fine old chap,

six foot, burly, legs apart, hands behind his back holding up the tails of his old macfarlane, Bolton at the window, grand old figure in his old red dressing-gown, back against the hangings, hand stretched out widening the chink, looking out, white world, great trouble, not a sound, only the embers, sound of dying, dying glow, Holloway, Bolton, Bolton, Holloway, old men, great trouble, white world, not a sound. (*Pause.*) Listen to it! (*Pause.*) Close your eyes and listen to it, what would you think it was? (*Pause. Vehement.*) A drip! A drip! (*Sound of drip, rapidly amplified, suddenly cut off.*) Again! (*Drip again. Amplification begins.*) No! (*Drip cut off. Pause.*) Father! (*Pause. Agitated.*) Stories, stories, years and years of stories, till the need came on me, for someone, to be with me, anyone, a stranger, to talk to, imagine he hears me, years of that, and then, now, for someone who . . . knew me, in the old days, anyone, to be with me, imagine he hears me, what I am, now. (*Pause.*) No good either.

(*Pause.*) Not there either. (*Pause.*) Try
again. (*Pause.*) White world, not a sound.
(*Pause.*) Holloway. (*Pause.*) Holloway
says he'll go, damned if he'll sit up all night
before a black grate, doesn't understand,
call a man out, an old friend, in the cold
and dark, an old friend, urgent need, bring
the bag, then not a word, no explanation,
no heat, no light, Bolton: "Please!
PLEASE!", Holloway, no refreshment, no
welcome, chilled to the medulla, catch his
death, can't understand, strange treatment,
old friend, says he'll go, doesn't move, not
a sound, fire dying, white beam from
window, ghastly scene, wishes to God he
hadn't come, no good, fire out, bitter cold,
great trouble, white world, not a sound, no
good. (*Pause.*) No good. (*Pause.*) Can't
do it. (*Pause.*) Listen to it! (*Pause.*)
Father! (*Pause.*) You wouldn't know me
now, you'd be sorry you ever had me, but
you were that already, a washout, that's
the last I heard from you, a washout.
(*Pause. Imitating father's voice.*) "Are you
coming for a dip?" "No." "Come on, come

on." "No." Glare, stump to door, turn, glare. "A washout, that's all you are, a washout!" (*Violent slam of door. Pause.*) Again! (*Slam. Pause.*) Slam life shut like that! (*Pause.*) Washout. (*Pause.*) Wish to Christ she had. (*Pause.*) Never met Ada, did you, or did you, I can't remember, no matter, no one'd know her now. (*Pause.*) What turned her against me do you think, the child I suppose, horrid little creature, wish to God we'd never had her, I used to walk with her in the fields, Jesus that was awful, she wouldn't let go my hand and I mad to talk. "Run along now, Addie, and look at the lambs." (*Imitating* ADDIE's *voice.*) "No papa." "Go on now, go on." (*Plaintive.*) "No papa." (*Violent.*) "Go on with you now when you're told and look at the lambs!" (ADDIE's *loud wail. Pause.*) Ada too, conversation with her, that was something, that's what hell will be like, small chat to the babbling of Lethe about the good old days when we wished we were dead. (*Pause.*) Price of margarine fifty years ago. (*Pause.*) And now. (*Pause.*

With solemn indignation.) Price of blue-band now! (*Pause.*) Father! (*Pause.*) Tired of talking to you. (*Pause.*) That was always the way, walk all over the mountains with you talking and talking and then suddenly mum and home in misery and not a word to a soul for weeks, sulky little bastard, better off dead, better off dead. (*Long pause.*) Ada. (*Pause. Louder.*) Ada!

ADA   (*low remote voice throughout*). Yes.

HENRY   Have you been there long?

ADA   Some little time. (*Pause.*) Why do you stop, don't mind me. (*Pause.*) Do you want me to go away? (*Pause.*) Where is Addie?

Pause.

HENRY   With her music master. (*Pause.*) Are you going to answer me today?

ADA   You shouldn't be sitting on the cold stones, they're bad for your growths. Raise yourself up till I slip my shawl under you. (*Pause.*) Is that better?

HENRY   No comparison, no comparison. (*Pause.*) Are you going to sit down beside me?

ADA   Yes. (*No sound as she sits.*) Like that? (*Pause.*) Or do you prefer like that? (*Pause.*) You don't care. (*Pause.*) Chilly enough I imagine, I hope you put on your jaegers. (*Pause.*) Did you put on your jaegers, Henry?

HENRY   What happened was this, I put them on and then I took them off again and then I put them on again and then I took them off again and then I took them on again and then I—

ADA   Have you them on now?

HENRY   I don't know. (*Pause.*) Hooves! (*Pause. Louder.*) Hooves! (*Sound of hooves walking on hard road. They die rapidly away.*) Again!

Hooves as before. Pause.

ADA   Did you hear them?

HENRY   Not well.

ADA   Galloping?

HENRY   No. (*Pause.*) Could a horse mark time?

Pause.

ADA   I'm not sure that I know what you mean.

HENRY   (*irritably*). Could a horse be trained to stand still and mark time with its four legs?

ADA   Oh. (*Pause.*) The ones I used to fancy all did. (*She laughs. Pause.*) Laugh, Henry, it's not every day I crack a joke. (*Pause.*) Laugh, Henry, do that for me.

HENRY   You wish *me* to laugh?

ADA   You laughed so charmingly once, I think that's what first attracted me to you. That and your smile. (*Pause.*) Come on, it will be like old times.

Pause. He tries to laugh, fails.

HENRY   Perhaps I should begin with the smile.

(*Pause for smile.*) Did that attract you?
(*Pause.*) Now I'll try again. (*Long horrible laugh.*) Any of the old charm there?

ADA   Oh Henry!

Pause.

HENRY   Listen to it! (*Pause.*) Lips and claws! (*Pause.*) Get away from it! Where it couldn't get at me! The Pampas! What?

ADA   Calm yourself.

HENRY   And I live on the brink of it! Why? Professional obligations? (*Brief laugh.*) Reasons of health? (*Brief laugh.*) Family ties? (*Brief laugh.*) A woman? (*Laugh in which she joins.*) Some old grave I cannot tear myself away from? (*Pause.*) Listen to it! What is it like?

ADA   It is like an old sound I used to hear. (*Pause.*) It is like another time, in the same place. (*Pause.*) It was rough, the spray came flying over us. (*Pause.*) Strange it should have been rough then.

(*Pause.*) And calm now.

Pause.

HENRY   Let us get up and go.

ADA   Go? Where? and Addie? She would be very distressed if she came and found you had gone without her. (*Pause.*) What do you suppose is keeping her?

Smart blow of cylindrical ruler on piano case. Unsteadily, ascending and descending, ADDIE *plays scale of A Flat Major, hands first together, then reversed. Pause.*

MUSIC MASTER   (*Italian accent*). Santa Cecilia!

Pause.

ADDIE   Will I play my piece now please?

Pause. MUSIC MASTER *beats two bars of waltz time with ruler on piano case.* ADDIE *plays opening bars of Chopin's 5th Waltz in A Flat Major.* MUSIC MASTER *beating time lightly with ruler as she plays. In first chord of bass, bar 5, she plays E instead of F. Resounding blow of ruler on piano case.*

ADDIE *stops playing.*

MUSIC MASTER	(*violently*). Fa!
ADDIE	(*tearfully*). What?
MUSIC MASTER	(*violently*). Eff! Eff!
ADDIE	(*tearfully*). Where?
MUSIC MASTER	(*violently*). Qua! (*He thumps note.*) Fa!

Pause. ADDIE *begins again,* MUSIC MASTER *beating time lightly with ruler. When she comes to bar 5 she makes same mistake. Tremendous blow of ruler on piano case.* ADDIE *stops playing, begins to wail.*

MUSIC MASTER   (*frenziedly*). Eff! Eff! (*He hammers note.*) Eff! (*He hammers note.*) Eff!

Hammered note, "eff" and ADDIE's *wail amplified to paroxysm, then suddenly cut off. Pause.*

ADA   You are silent today.

HENRY   It was not enough to drag her into the world, now she must play the piano.

ADA   She must learn. She shall learn. That—and
          riding.

          Hooves walking.

RIDING MASTER   Now Miss! Elbows in Miss! Hands down
          Miss! (*Hooves trotting.*) Now Miss! Back
          straight Miss! Knees in Miss! (*Hooves
          cantering.*) Now Miss! Tummy in Miss!
          Chin up Miss! (*Hooves galloping.*) Now
          Miss! Eyes front Miss! (ADDIE *begins to
          wail.*) Now Miss! Now Miss!

          Galloping hooves, "now Miss!" and ADDIE'S
          *wail amplified to paroxysm, then suddenly
          cut off. Pause.*

ADA   What are you thinking of? (*Pause.*) I was
          never taught, until it was too late. All my
          life I regretted it.

HENRY   What was your strong point, I forget.

ADA   Oh . . . geometry I suppose, plane and
          solid. (*Pause.*) First plane, then solid.
          (*Shingle as he gets up.*) Why do you
          get up?

HENRY   I thought I might try and get as far as the water's edge. (*Pause. With a sigh.*) And back. (*Pause.*) Stretch my old bones.

Pause.

ADA   Well why don't you? (*Pause.*) Don't stand there thinking about it. (*Pause.*) Don't stand there staring. (*Pause. He goes towards sea. Boots on shingle, say ten steps. He halts at water's edge. Pause. Sea a little louder. Distant.*) Don't wet your good boots.

Pause.

HENRY   Don't, don't . . .

Sea suddenly rough.

ADA   (*twenty years earlier, imploring*). Don't! Don't!

HENRY   (*do., urgent*). Darling!

ADA   (*do., more feebly*). Don't!

HENRY   (*do., exultantly*). Darling!

Rough sea. ADA cries out. Cry and sea

amplified, cut off. End of evocation. Pause.
Sea calm. He goes back up deeply shelving
beach. Boots laborious on shingle. He
halts. Pause. He moves on. He halts. Pause.
Sea calm and faint.

ADA   Don't sit there gaping. Sit down. (*Pause.*
Shingle as he sits.) On the shawl. (*Pause.*)
Are you afraid we might touch? (*Pause.*)
Henry.

HENRY   Yes.

ADA   You should see a doctor about your talking,
it's worse, what must it be like for Addie?
(*Pause.*) Do you know what she said to me
once, when she was still quite small, she
said, Mummy, why does Daddy keep on
talking all the time? She heard you in the
lavatory. I didn't know what to answer.

HENRY   Daddy! Addie! (*Pause.*) I told you to tell
her I was praying. (*Pause.*) Roaring
prayers at God and his saints.

ADA   It's very bad for the child. (*Pause.*) It's
silly to say it keeps you from hearing it, it

doesn't keep you from hearing it and even if it does you shouldn't be hearing it, there must be something wrong with your brain.

Pause.

HENRY   That! I shouldn't be hearing that!

ADA   I don't think you are hearing it. And if you are what's wrong with it, it's a lovely peaceful gentle soothing sound, why do you hate it? (*Pause.*) And if you hate it why don't you keep away from it? Why are you always coming down here? (*Pause.*) There's something wrong with your brain, you ought to see Holloway, he's alive still, isn't he?

Pause.

HENRY   (*wildly*). Thuds, I want thuds! Like this! (*He fumbles in the shingle, catches up two big stones and starts dashing them together.*) Stone! (*Clash.*) Stone! (*Clash. "Stone!" and clash amplified, cut off. Pause. He throws one stone away. Sound of its fall.*) That's life! (*He throws the other*

stone away. Sound of its fall.) Not this . . .
(*pause*) . . . sucking!

ADA And why life? (*Pause.*) Why life, Henry?
(*Pause.*) Is there anyone about?

HENRY Not a living soul.

ADA I thought as much. (*Pause.*) When we
longed to have it to ourselves there was
always someone. Now that it does not
matter the place is deserted.

HENRY Yes, you were always very sensitive to
being seen in gallant conversation. The
least feather of smoke on the horizon and
you adjusted your dress and became
immersed in the Manchester Guardian.
(*Pause.*) The hole is still there, after all
these years. (*Pause. Louder.*) The hole is
still there.

ADA What hole? The earth is full of holes.

HENRY Where we did it at last for the first time.

ADA Ah yes, I think I remember. (*Pause.*) The
place has not changed.

HENRY   Oh yes it has, *I* can see it. (*Confidentially.*)
There is a levelling going on! (*Pause.*)
What age is she now?

ADA   I have lost count of time.

HENRY   Twelve? Thirteen? (*Pause.*) Fourteen?

ADA   I really could not tell you, Henry.

HENRY   It took us a long time to have her. (*Pause.*)
Years we kept hammering away at it.
(*Pause.*) But we did it in the end. (*Pause.
Sigh.*) We had her in the end. (*Pause.*)
Listen to it! (*Pause.*) It's not so bad when
you get out on it. (*Pause.*) Perhaps I
should have gone into the merchant navy.

ADA   It's only on the surface, you know.
Underneath all is as quiet as the grave. Not
a sound. All day, all night, not a sound.

Pause.

HENRY   Now I walk about with the gramophone.
But I forgot it today.

ADA   There is no sense in that. (*Pause.*) There
is no sense in trying to drown it. (*Pause.*)

See Holloway.

Pause.

HENRY   Let us go for a row.

ADA   A row? And Addie? She would be very distressed if she came and found you had gone for a row without her. (*Pause.*) Who were you with just now? (*Pause.*) Before you spoke to me.

HENRY   I was trying to be with my father.

ADA   Oh. (*Pause.*) No difficulty about that.

HENRY   I mean I was trying to get him to be with me. (*Pause.*) You seem a little cruder than usual today, Ada. (*Pause.*) I was asking him if he ever met you, I couldn't remember.

ADA   Well?

HENRY   He doesn't answer any more.

ADA   I suppose you have worn him out. (*Pause.*) You wore him out living and now you are wearing him out dead. (*Pause.*) The time comes when one cannot speak to you any more. (*Pause.*) The time will come when no one will speak to you at all, not even complete strangers. (*Pause.*) You will be quite alone with your voice, there will be no other voice in the world but yours. (*Pause.*) Do you hear me?

Pause.

HENRY   I can't remember if he met you.

ADA   You know he met me.

HENRY   No, Ada, I don't know, I'm sorry, I have forgotten almost everything connected with you.

ADA   You weren't there. Just your mother and sister. I had called to fetch you, as arranged. We were to go bathing together.

Pause.

HENRY   (*irritably*). Drive on, drive on! Why do people always stop in the middle of what they are saying?

ADA   None of them knew where you were. Your bed had not been slept in. They were all shouting at one another. Your sister said she would throw herself off the cliff. Your father got up and went out, slamming the door. I left soon afterwards and passed him on the road. He did not see me. He was sitting on a rock looking out to sea. I never forgot his posture. And yet it was a common one. You used to have it sometimes. Perhaps just the stillness, as if he had been turned to stone. I could never make it out.

Pause.

HENRY   Keep on, keep on! (*Imploringly.*) Keep it going, Ada, every syllable is a second gained.

ADA   That's all, I'm afraid. (*Pause.*) Go on now with your father or your stories or whatever you were doing, don't mind me any more.

HENRY   I can't! (*Pause.*) I can't do it any more!

ADA   You were doing it a moment ago, before you spoke to me.

HENRY   (*angrily*). I can't do it any more now! (*Pause.*) Christ!

Pause.

ADA   Yes, you know what I mean, there are
      attitudes remain in one's mind for reasons
      that are clear, the carriage of a head for
      example, bowed when one would have
      thought it should be lifted, and vice versa,
      or a hand suspended in mid air, as if
      unowned. That kind of thing. But with
      your father sitting on the rock that day
      nothing of the kind, no detail you could
      put your finger on and say, How very
      peculiar! No, I could never make it out.
      Perhaps, as I said, just the great stillness of
      the whole body, as if all the breath had
      left it. (*Pause.*) Is this rubbish a help to
      you, Henry? (*Pause.*) I can try and go on
      a little if you wish. (*Pause.*) No? (*Pause.*)
      Then I think I'll be getting back.

HENRY Not yet! You needn't speak. Just listen.
      Not even. Be with me. (*Pause.*) Ada!
      (*Pause. Louder.*) Ada! (*Pause.*) Christ!
      (*Pause.*) Hooves! (*Pause. Louder.*) Hooves!
      (*Pause.*) Christ! (*Long pause.*) Left soon
      afterwards, passed you on the road, didn't
      see her, looking out to . . . (*Pause.*) Can't
      have been looking out to sea. (*Pause.*)

Unless you had gone round the other side.
(*Pause.*) Had you gone round the
cliff side? (*Pause.*) Father! (*Pause.*) Must
have I suppose. (*Pause.*) Stands watching
you a moment, then on down path to tram,
up on open top and sits down in front.
(*Pause.*) Sits down in front. (*Pause.*)
Suddenly feels uneasy and gets down
again, conductor: "Changed your mind,
Miss?", goes back up path, no sign of you.
(*Pause.*) Very unhappy and uneasy, hangs
round a bit, not a soul about, cold wind
coming in off sea, goes back down path
and takes tram home. (*Pause.*) Takes tram
home. (*Pause.*) Christ! (*Pause.*) "My dear
Bolton . . ." (*Pause.*) "If it's an injection
you want, Bolton, let down your trousers
and I'll give you one, I have a panhyster-
ectomy at nine," meaning of course the
anaesthetic. (*Pause.*) Fire out, bitter cold,
white world, great trouble, not a sound.
(*Pause.*) Bolton starts playing with the
curtain, no, hanging, difficult to describe,
draws it back, no, kind of gathers it
towards him and the moon comes flooding
in, then lets it fall back, heavy velvet

affair, and pitch black in the room, then towards him again, white, black, white, black, Holloway: "Stop that for the love of God, Bolton, do you want to finish me?" (*Pause.*) Black, white, black, white, maddening thing. (*Pause.*) Then he suddenly strikes a match, Bolton does, lights a candle, catches it up above his head, walks over and looks Holloway full in the eye. (*Pause.*) Not a word, just the look, the old blue eye, very glassy, lids worn thin, lashes gone, whole thing swimming, and the candle shaking over his head. (*Pause.*) Tears? (*Pause. Long laugh.*) Good God no! (*Pause.*) Not a word, just the look, the old blue eye, Holloway: "If you want a shot say so and let me get to hell out of here." (*Pause.*) "We've had this before, Bolton, don't ask me to go through it again." (*Pause.*) Bolton: "Please!" (*Pause.*) "Please!" (*Pause.*) "Please, Holloway!" (*Pause.*) Candle shaking and guttering all over the place, lower now, old arm tired, takes it in the other hand and holds it high again, that's it, that was always it, night, and the embers cold, and the glim shaking

in your old fist, saying, Please! Please!
(*Pause.*) Begging. (*Pause.*) Of the poor.
(*Pause.*) Ada! (*Pause.*) Father! (*Pause.*)
Christ! (*Pause.*) Holds it high again,
naughty world, fixes Holloway, eyes
drowned, won't ask again, just the look,
Holloway covers his face, not a sound,
white world, bitter cold, ghastly scene, old
men, great trouble, no good. (*Pause.*) No
good. (*Pause.*) Christ! (*Pause. Shingle as
he gets up. He goes towards sea. Boots on
shingle. He halts. Pause. Sea a little
louder.*) On. (*Pause. He moves on. Boots
on shingle. He halts at water's edge.
Pause. Sea a little louder.*) Little book.
(*Pause.*) This evening . . . (*Pause.*)
Nothing this evening. (*Pause.*) Tomorrow
. . . tomorrow . . . plumber at nine, then
nothing. (*Pause. Puzzled.*) Plumber at
nine? (*Pause.*) Ah yes, the waste. (*Pause.*)
Words. (*Pause.*) Saturday . . . nothing.
Sunday . . . Sunday . . . nothing all day.
(*Pause.*) Nothing, all day nothing. (*Pause.*)
All day all night nothing. (*Pause.*) Not
a sound.

Sea.

Act
Without
Words I

A MIME FOR
ONE PLAYER

**Translated from the
French by the author**

Act Without Words I (*Acte sans Paroles*) was first performed at the Royal Court Theatre in London on April 3, 1957. It was directed and performed by Deryk Mendel, the decor was designed by Jacques Noel and the music composed by John Beckett.

Desert. Dazzling light.

The man is flung backwards on stage from right wing. He falls, gets up immediately, dusts himself, turns aside, reflects.

Whistle from right wing.

He reflects, goes out right.

Immediately flung back on stage he falls, gets up immediately, dusts himself, turns aside, reflects.

Whistle from left wing.

He reflects, goes out left.

Immediately flung back on stage he falls, gets up immediately, dusts himself, turns aside, reflects.

Whistle from left wing.

He reflects, goes towards left wing, hesitates, thinks better of it, halts, turns aside, reflects.

125

A little tree descends from flies, lands. It has a single bough some three yards from ground and at its summit a meager tuft of palms casting at its foot a circle of shadow.

He continues to reflect.

Whistle from above.

He turns, sees tree, reflects, goes to it, sits down in its shadow, looks at his hands.

A pair of tailor's scissors descends from flies, comes to rest before tree, a yard from ground.

He continues to look at his hands.

Whistle from above.

He looks up, sees scissors, takes them and starts to trim his nails.

The palms close like a parasol, the shadow disappears.

He drops scissors, reflects.

A tiny carafe, to which is attached a huge label inscribed WATER, descends from flies, comes to rest some three yards from ground.

He continues to reflect.

Whistle from above.

He looks up, sees carafe, reflects, gets up, goes and stands under it, tries in vain to reach it, renounces, turns aside, reflects.

A big cube descends from flies, lands.

He continues to reflect.

Whistle from above.

He turns, sees cube, looks at it, at carafe, reflects, goes to cube, takes it up, carries it over and sets it down under carafe, tests its stability, gets up on it, tries in vain to reach carafe, renounces, gets down, carries cube back to its place, turns aside, reflects.

A second smaller cube descends from flies, lands.

He continues to reflect.

Whistle from above.

He turns, sees second cube, looks at it, at carafe, goes to second cube, takes it up, carries it over and sets it down under carafe, tests its stability, gets up on it, tries in vain to reach carafe, renounces, gets down, takes up second cube to carry it back to its place, hesitates, thinks better of it, sets it down, goes to big cube, takes it up, carries it over and puts it on small one, tests their stability, gets up on them, the cubes collapse, he falls, gets up immediately, brushes himself, reflects.

He takes up small cube, puts it on big one, tests their stability, gets up on them and is about to reach carafe when it is pulled up a little way and comes to rest beyond his reach.

He gets down, reflects, carries cubes back to their place, one by one, turns aside, reflects.

A third still smaller cube descends from flies, lands.

He continues to reflect.

Whistle from above.

He turns, sees third cube, looks at it,
reflects, turns aside, reflects.

The third cube is pulled up and disappears
in flies.

Beside carafe a rope descends from flies,
with knots to facilitate ascent.

He continues to reflect.

Whistle from above.

He turns, sees rope, reflects, goes to it,
climbs up it and is about to reach carafe
when rope is let out and deposits him
back on ground.

He reflects, looks around for scissors, sees
them, goes and picks them up, returns to
rope and starts to cut it with scissors.

The rope is pulled up, lifts him off ground,
he hangs on, succeeds in cutting rope,
falls back on ground, drops scissors, falls,

gets up again immediately, brushes
himself, reflects.

The rope is pulled up quickly and
disappears in flies.

With length of rope in his possession he
makes a lasso with which he tries to
lasso carafe.

The carafe is pulled up quickly and
disappears in flies.

He turns aside, reflects.

He goes with lasso in his hand to tree,
looks at bough, turns and looks at cubes,
looks again at bough, drops lasso, goes to
cubes, takes up small one, carries it over
and sets it down under bough, goes back
for big one, takes it up and carries it over
under bough, makes to put it on small one,
hesitates, thinks better of it, sets it down,
takes up small one and puts it on big one,
tests their stability, turns aside and stoops
to pick up lasso.

The bough folds down against trunk.

He straightens up with lasso in his hand,
turns and sees what has happened.

He drops lasso, turns aside, reflects.

He carries back cubes to their place, one
by one, goes back for lasso, carries it over
to cubes and lays it in a neat coil on
small one.

He turns aside, reflects.

Whistle from right wing.

He reflects, goes out right.

Immediately flung back on stage he falls,
gets up immediately, brushes himself,
turns aside, reflects.

Whistle from left wing.

He does not move.

He looks at his hands, looks around for
scissors, sees them, goes and picks them
up, starts to trim his nails, stops, reflects,
runs his finger along blade of scissors,
goes and lays them on small cube, turns

aside, opens his collar, frees his neck
and fingers it.

The small cube is pulled up and
disappears in flies, carrying away rope
and scissors.

He turns to take scissors, sees what has
happened.

He turns aside, reflects.

He goes and sits down on big cube.

The big cube is pulled from under him.
He falls. The big cube is pulled up and
disappears in flies.

He remains lying on his side, his face
towards auditorium, staring before him.

The carafe descends from flies and comes
to rest a few feet from his body.

He does not move.

Whistle from above.

He does not move.

The carafe descends further, dangles and
plays about his face.

He does not move.

The carafe is pulled up and disappears
in flies.

The bough returns to horizontal,
the palms open, the shadow returns.

Whistle from above.

He does not move.

The tree is pulled up and disappears in
flies.

He looks at his hands.

CURTAIN

Act
Without
Words II

A MIME FOR
TWO PLAYERS

Translated from the
French by the author

NOTE   This mime should be played on a low and narrow platform at back of stage, violently lit in its entire length, the rest of the stage being in darkness. Frieze effect.

A is slow, awkward (gags dressing and undressing), absent. B brisk, rapid, precise. The two actions therefore, though B has more to do than A, should have approximately the same duration.

ARGUMENT   Beside each other on ground, two yards from right wing, two sacks, A's and B's, A's being to right (as seen from auditorium) of B's, i.e. nearer right wing. On ground beside sack B a little pile of clothes (C) neatly folded (coat and trousers surmounted by boots and hat).

Enter goad right, strictly horizontal. The point stops a foot short of sack A. Pause. The point draws back, pauses, darts forward into sack, withdraws, recoils to a foot short of sack. Pause. The sack does not move. The point draws back

137

again, a little further than before, pauses,
darts forward again into sack, withdraws,
recoils to a foot short of sack. Pause. The
sack moves. Exit goad.

A, wearing shirt, crawls out of sack, halts,
broods, prays, broods, gets to his feet,
broods, takes a little bottle of pills from
his shirt pocket, broods, swallows a pill,
puts bottle back, broods, goes to clothes,
broods, puts on clothes, broods, takes a
large partly eaten carrot from coat pocket,
bites off a piece, chews an instant, spits it
out with disgust, puts carrot back, broods,
picks up two sacks, carries them bowed
and staggering on his back half way to
left wing, sets them down, broods, takes
off clothes (except shirt), lets them fall
in an untidy heap, broods, takes another
pill, broods, kneels, prays, crawls into sack
and lies still, sack A being now to left
of sack B.

Pause.

Enter goad right on wheeled support (one

wheel). The point stops a foot short of
sack B. Pause. The point draws back,
pauses, darts forward into sack, withdraws,
recoils to a foot short of sack. Pause.
The sack moves. Exit goad.

B, wearing shirt, crawls out of sack, gets
to his feet, takes from shirt pocket and
consults a large watch, puts watch back,
does exercises, consults watch, takes a
tooth brush from shirt pocket and brushes
teeth vigorously, puts brush back, rubs
scalp vigorously, takes a comb from shirt
pocket and combs hair, puts comb back,
consults watch, goes to clothes, puts them
on, consults watch, takes a brush from
coat pocket and brushes clothes
vigorously, brushes hair vigorously, puts
brush back, takes a little mirror from
coat pocket and inspects appearance, puts
mirror back, takes carrot from coat pocket,
bites off a piece, chews and swallows with
appetite, puts carrot back, consults watch,
takes a map from coat pocket and consults
it, puts map back, consults watch, takes a

compass from coat pocket and consults it,
puts compass back, consults watch, picks
up two sacks and carries them bowed and
staggering on his back to two yards short
of left wing, sets them down, consults
watch, takes off clothes (except shirt),
folds them in a neat pile, consults watch,
does exercises, consults watch, rubs scalp,
combs hair, brushes teeth, consults and
winds watch, crawls into sack and lies
still, sack B being now to left of sack A
as originally.

Pause.

Enter goad right on wheeled support
(two wheels). The point stops a foot short
of sack A. Pause. The point draws back,
pauses, darts forward into sack.
withdraws, recoils to a foot short of sack.
Pause. The sack does not move. The
point draws back again, a little further
than before, pauses, darts forward again
into sack, withdraws, recoils to a foot short
of sack. Pause. The sack moves.

Exit goad.

A crawls out of sack, halts, broods, prays.

CURTAIN

POSITION I

C B A ←

POSITION II

C A B ←

POSITION III

C B A ←

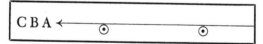

STAGE FRONT